MW00811396

AOMORI

AKITA

NORTHERN
AREA

● Akita
78

IWATE

H O N S H Ū

YAMAGATA

MIYAGI

Yamagata 79 ●

● Sendai 81–84

Yonezawa
80 ●

Niigata 87 ●
Nagaoka 86 ●

FUKUSHIMA

Toyama 101

NIIGATA

● Kōriyama 85

Maebashi

AMA

Matsumoto
89

TOCHIGI

Utsunomiya

Karuizawa 88

GUNMA

IBARAKI

NAGANO

SAITAMA

Tsukuba

99

YAMANASHI

TOKYO

Urawa
Chiba

SHIZUOKA

KANAGAWA

CHIBA

ka 91–92 ●

Iamamatsu 93

–96

Mishima 90

Yokohama

97

CENTRAL AREA

TOKYO AND
THE KANTŌ AREA

TOKYO	1–27
KANAGAWA	28–35
CHIBA	36–39
SAITAMA	40–45
TOCHIGI	46–47
IBARAKI	48–49
GUNMA	50–54

OKINAWA

FLEA MARKETS OF JAPAN

FLEA MARKETS OF JAPAN

A Pocket Guide for Antique Buyers

THEODORE MANNING

KODANSHA INTERNATIONAL
Tokyo · New York · London

The publisher would like to express its gratitude to the Japan Folk Crafts Museum (Nihon Mingei-kan) in Tokyo for granting permission to reproduce images from its collection.

Illustrations by Noriko Murotani

Distributed in the United States by Kodansha America, Inc., 575 Lexington Avenue, New York, N.Y. 10022, and in the United Kingdom and continental Europe by Kodansha Europe Ltd., 95 Aldwych, London WC2B 4JF.

Published by Kodansha International Ltd., 17–14, Otowa 1-chome, Bunkyo-ku, Tokyo 112–8652, and Kodansha America, Inc.

First edition, 2003
ISBN 4–7700–2902–0
03 04 05 06 07 08 09 10   10 9 8 7 6 5 4 3 2 1

www.thejapanpage.com

C O N T E N T S

I. BEFORE GOING SHOPPING

Background
A Brief History of Flea Markets ▪ Availability, Quality, and Prices of Antiques ▪ Advantages of Flea Markets ▪ Annoyances and Risks

Behind the Scenes
Flea-Market Vendors ▪ Vendor Profile ▪ Sources of Antiques ▪ Establishment of New Flea Markets

II. SHOPPING GUIDELINES

III. FLEA MARKET LISTINGS

Your forearms ripple with goosebumps and your heart takes a little leap—these are the frissons of expectation before a first date, your first pay raise, or your first trip abroad. They also describe what happens to many people en route to a flea market. Those few minutes of anticipation as they head toward the market are exciting in a special way. What will I find today? What treasures will I uncover? Will I find any real bargains?

The pleasure of the hunt effects one and all, but more so if you are a thing person. What's a thing person? Simply put, it is a person with a love for objects that have a certain charm or character. I can best explain it by way of illustration. Once a visitor to my house looked around at all the objects lining my shelves and decorating the walls and said, "Boy, you sure have a lot of stuff." Indeed I do, but it is more than just stuff. What my guest failed to see is that every one of the artifacts on display was chosen. Each entered my life as the result of a fascination with special things—a curiosity about their history, their use, and how they were made. My visitor, an unthing person, saw them as mere clutter. He had no appreciation for the objects' beauty, grace, or presence.

Thing people are usually in search of an antique that resonates with a sense of time and place. There are probably lots of reasons why artifacts should appeal to some people and not others, but the whys and wherefores are less important than the act of immersing oneself in the free-flowing, high-spirited swirl of a flea market. Interacting with objects of different shapes and colors and materials and periods, all made by craftspeople decades or even centuries ago, is a pleasure we should all treat ourselves to at least once. It is a visual and sensual feast that gives nourishment to some hungry part of the psyche. And should you find a treasure, it will, like a new friend, become a part of your life.

The stuff at flea markets includes antiques and castoffs and everything in between. The sellers are usually professional dealers. While few of them are scholars or researchers, they are generally well informed about what they sell, especially since approximately half of them have their own antique stores. In many cases, you can talk to them at length and in great detail about what they sell. Talking to dealers, of any level of knowledge, can only enrich your experience.

Once you find a specialty or interest, you will soon find vendors with the same focus and may naturally drift into a friendship with them. The best vendors, after they learn of your interests and tastes, will take pleasure in finding something that may add to or fill a hole in your budding collection.

So join the hunt. Rise to the chase. Make the rounds and go where your curiosity leads. Don't be afraid to touch, smell, or heft the objects you find. That is part of the allure of the flea-market experience in Japan. With a few trips under your belt, if you find yourself changing from casual observer to inveterate flea-market shopper to hard-core collector, know that you are in for a thrilling ride.

With this book, you are well on your way. Theodore Manning has done a heroic job of filling a need. As far as I know, this is the first and only book ever written with the specific needs of flea-market shoppers in mind, and it is destined to be a classic. So keep it close at hand—and happy hunting.

K. B. Booth

INTRODUCTION

For the last thirty years, too many foreigners, myself included, have fumbled through the flea markets of Japan—enthusiastically but awkwardly, gamely but ignorantly—looking for Japanese antiques to call their own. We usually managed to buy and pay for what we wanted, but unable to speak the language, unaware of what we were looking at, and unused to the unique style of flea-market commerce, we often got it wrong, upsetting the vendors, demeaning the merchandise, and managing to embarrass ourselves in the process.

With the release of this book, those days are over. *Flea Markets of Japan: A Pocket Guide for Antique Buyers* contains virtually everything I have learned in over ten years of browsing, bargaining, and buying antiques at flea markets. It gives you the information, insight, and linguistic tools you need to shop smart, almost from day one, without making the mistakes most of us fell prey to in the past.

Of course, "shopping smart" means different things to different people, but it comes down to knowing how to get the merchandise you want, at the price you want, whether you are a souvenir shopper, a collector, an interior designer, a sourcing agent, an antique dealer, an exhibit curator, or an artist seeking new materials to work with.

I am what you could call a do-it-yourself decorator, so to me shopping smart means finding something that will give my home an unmistakably Japanese touch. But it must be something large enough to have a strong visual impact, and it has to fit my definition of "affordable," which means less than $500.

Once I found a *tairyō-bata*, a large Japanese fishing-boat banner flown on return to port to announce a successful catch. Big enough to fill the wall of my living room, with bright colors and a bold design depicting a boat at sea, this unusual item stops visitors in their tracks. It cost less than $100. A more expensive item is the long, low-slung shopkeeper's desk (*o-tanazukue*) gracing my entryway. Used by the owner of a pharmacy some one hundred years ago, it doubled as an indoor billboard by incorporating in its front facing an eye-catching advertisement for a brand of eye medicine. This attention-grabber set me back about $450.

I especially like to find old or obsolete items that can be used in ways not originally intended; that way, I not only get to show off the objects but also display the ingenuity with which they have been put to use. A few years ago I bought an old wooden hoe (*kuwa*). Having no use for the handle, I discarded it. But I kept the head to use as a sort of desktop organizer. About 20 inches (50 centimeters) long, with more than twenty 3-inch (7-centimeter) -long "teeth," it is perfect for the task of holding letters, postcards, and photographs. I use a blue-and-white porcelain charcoal brazier (*hibachi*) as either an ice bucket or a wine cooler, and a wooden box with holes in the bottom, once used to make *tofu*, as a self-draining flower box. I turned the frame of a foot warmer (*kotatsu yagura*) into the base of a coffee table.

But that's just me. Many shoppers are content with smaller items, such as the avidly collected *soba-choko*, ceramic cups used to hold the sauce for buckwheat noodles. Shoppers with a larger budget often seek out wooden chests or Japanese ceramics.

Whatever your tastes or budget, the information in these pages—the shopping guidelines, list of things to buy, and "flea-market Japanese"—will make your experience that much more enjoyable. With *Flea Markets of Japan* in hand, you will shop smarter—and more successfully—than we did in the old days.

In all your shopping excursions, I wish you the best of luck.

ACKNOWLEDGMENTS

It would have been impossible to write this book without the close cooperation of Masae (Mako) Arai.

Arai-san made several important contributions, among which were compiling the flea-market listings, making contact with flea-market organizers, getting press passes for several flea markets, reviewing the Flea-Market Japanese section for completeness and accuracy, and checking the names, origins, and uses of items selected for inclusion in the Things to Buy section.

She made an equally important, albeit intangible, contribution by providing companionship and camaraderie over the course of the four months during which the book was written.

Mako, you have my sincerest thanks.

■　■　■

For kindly granting permission to take photographs, thanks go to the organizers and vendors of the following Kanto-area flea markets: Heiwajima Zenkoku Komingu Kottō Matsuri (held at Tokyo Ryūtsū Center) and Kottō Jamboree (held at Tokyo International Exhibition Center).

Thanks also go to Keiko Nakano, owner of Gallery Torisumi in Jiyūgaoka, Setagaya-ku, Tokyo, for allowing me to take photographs of numerous items from among her spectacular inventory of kimono, *obi*, and accessories.

■　■　■

Finally, I would like to express my gratitude towards John Adair, proprietor of Kurofune, located in the Roppongi section of Tokyo. A dealer specializing in the highest-quality Japanese antique furniture and prints, Mr. Adair provided invaluable behind-the-scenes insight into the world of antique sourcing agents, wholesalers, and auctioneers.

1. BEFORE GOING
SHOPPING

BACKGROUND

A Brief History of Flea Markets

The flea market is a comparatively recent addition to Japanese society. Although a few flea markets were established well over a hundred years ago—the market held at Tōji Temple in Kyoto, for instance, dates from before the Edo period (1603–1868)—the vast majority has come into existence since 1975. This blossoming of flea markets has been fertilized not only by Japan's affluence but also by the development of a buyer-collector culture among antique enthusiasts; traditionally, the buying and collecting of antiques was for the most part done by museums and a few wealthy patrons of the arts.

The number of new flea markets has gradually increased since the 1970s, with a surge from the mid-1990s. One reason frequently cited for the current increase in popularity of flea markets is that after a long love affair with everything foreign, the Japanese have rekindled their affection for the traditional Japanese object.

Availability, Quality, and Prices of Antiques

The heightened popularity of flea markets has led to rapidly rising antique prices—especially for high-quality items—even as it has brought about an increase in the number of antiques in circulation.

Prices overall are rising by an estimated 10 to 15 percent each year, and for the most popular types of antiques, such as ceramics and textiles, annual price increases are on the order of 15 to 20 percent.

The implication for shoppers is clear: if you see something you like, buy it immediately. It is only going to get more expensive. Besides, if you put off purchasing something that catches your eye, you risk losing it to someone who didn't wait.

There is another reason to be in a hurry to purchase. Regardless of the increase in the number of antiques, high-quality antiques are increasingly difficult to find. Greater demand for antiques has meanwhile pulled more items of average or below-average quality onto the market. This, in turn, has made it more important that a shopper be well informed and know how to get information from flea-market vendors and antique dealers.

Advantages of Flea Markets

Flea markets offer several clear advantages over antique shops. These include:

- lower prices (recent price increases notwithstanding)
- the availability of a wider variety of merchandise in one place
- flexible pricing (bargaining is allowed)
- a more relaxed atmosphere
- the chance to encounter merchandise rarely appearing in antique shops (bric-a-brac and other obscure or one-off items impossible for store owners to stock regularly are some of the real finds)
- a pleasant day's outing (especially for outdoor markets)

Flea markets also tend to be more exciting than antique shops owing to their bustling, convivial atmosphere.

Annoyances and Risks

Shopping at flea markets is in most respects thoroughly pleasant, and for many visitors browsing affords as much pleasure as making an actual purchase. However, there are certain annoyances and risks of which to be aware:

- crowds and the hassles that go with them—although this is nothing new to residents of Japanese cities
- the lack of facilities or amenities, especially at outdoor markets—no parking, no toilets, no concessions, no drinking fountains, few trash cans
- no smoking, a rule enforced even at outdoor markets
- vendors with a condescending attitude towards foreigners, based on the assumption that all non-Japanese are ignorant of Japanese culture and cannot speak a word of Japanese
- vendors who try to charge unreasonably high prices (although this is uncommon)
- vendors who falsely represent merchandise, be it disguising a defect or exaggerating an item's age (although this is uncommon)

Yet, these things are precisely what a true bazaar is all about—free-wheeling atmosphere, and the kind of charm that comes from a bit of chaos.

BEHIND THE SCENES

Flea-Market Vendors

All flea-market vendors are licensed dealers of antiques. By current estimates, there are some 4,000 to 5,000 active vendors, although the number of licensed dealers, which includes antique-shop owners and others in the antique world not directly involved in selling at flea markets, is much higher. Flea-market vendors often own stores, usually in a provincial town or city, though many are itinerant vendors, selling only at flea markets.

Flea-market vendors spend much of their time on the move, driving from one venue to the next. Many seem to have developed a local or regional circuit, appearing regularly at the venues of their choice within a reasonable driving distance from their homes. But other vendors are less tied to one location, so shoppers should not assume that a seller appearing at a certain flea market one month will be there the next—another risk of deferring a purchase. Less frequently, vendors travel longer distances in search of more potential customers at the larger flea markets staged intermittently around Japan.

Like craftspeople and aficionados of many kinds, flea-market vendors form a loose nationwide network, operating in a small world of their own. People working on the same circuit are often well acquainted, or at least know *of* each other. They also come into contact with each other at the larger flea markets, which tend to draw antique sellers from wider areas.

An organizer runs each flea market. The organizer (who is often a vendor as well) is responsible for finding and booking the venue, signing up sellers and collecting participation fees, allotting space, and promoting the flea market.

Vendors are required to pay fees to flea-market organizers, commonly in the form of rent for the space to set up displays; naturally, the larger the space, the higher the fee. Fees for indoor flea markets tend to be much higher than those for outdoor flea markets, because renting space at exhibition centers and other indoor venues costs much more than using the grounds of a shrine or temple. Indoor flea markets usually last two or three days, whereas outdoor flea markets are usually one-day events.

Vendor Profile

The typical vendor is a man aged between 35 and 65; the far fewer numbers of female traders tend to be in the same age range. The flea-market vendor's lifestyle is in many ways the antithesis of the company employee's, as flea-market selling is a job that generates little income, carries low status, affords no security, and offers no prospect of advancement. Those in the business are content not to belong to a large organization and comfortable with a somewhat nomadic lifestyle.

It is not that all vendors are nonconformists, but the terms "offbeat" or "unconventional" could be applied in some degree to most. There are obvious indicators, like beards and long hair, as well as more subtle manifestations, such as a relaxed and informal manner and an almost nonchalant way of addressing customers.

While most vendors have a personality suited to the job of selling antiques, not all are true antique enthusiasts—or at least they don't always act like it. A fairly large number of traders don't appear particularly interested in the merchandise they are selling, and judging from their tentative responses to questions about an item's age, origins, and uses, they don't make a serious effort to get information, either.

Sources of Antiques

There are several ways for sellers to obtain antiques. Most antiques are acquired at auctions, which are open only to licensed dealers. Vendors sometimes buy antiques from wholesalers or dealers, who also shop at auctions but who are able to buy in bulk for a lower unit cost. Vendors occasionally buy antiques from private individuals, often obtaining things about to be thrown out.

Sellers of antiques tend to treat them as mere commodities. In this sense they are no different than any other retailers, brokers, or professional resellers, trying to earn a reasonable profit by pricing their merchandise well above cost. Moreover, they are understandably reluctant to let shoppers know where and how merchandise was obtained (even if fears of leading shoppers to the source are exaggerated), and little is to be gained from pressing for this kind of information.

Establishment of New Flea Markets

In response to a surge in the popularity of flea-market shopping, scores of new flea markets have been established in recent years. The organizers of flea markets have accommodated the increased number of shoppers—and the vendors who serve them—by opening up new venues. Traders who for all intents and purposes were locked out of existing locations due to a *de facto* monopoly of the space by established vendors have also set up new flea markets. Assuming the current popularity of flea-market shopping continues, it seems safe to say that many more flea markets will be established in the years to come.

II. SHOPPING GUIDELINES

This chapter explains the unwritten rules of flea-market shopping, then gives hints on how to bargain, how to get the lowest price, how to find out more about an item, and other helpful advice. Over time, you will pick up most of these things on your own, but the guidelines presented here will hopefully help you learn more quickly.

SHOPPING PROTOCOL

One of the most important elements of shopping protocol—and one of the most appealing aspects of flea-market shopping—is that browsing is both allowed and encouraged. Just walk up and check out what's for sale. You can look at whatever you want, for as long you want, without in any way upsetting or annoying vendors. Also, unless merchandise is marked to the contrary, assume it is okay to touch or handle it. If it isn't, a little sign, probably handwritten, will say "Do Not Touch" (*sawaranai de kudasai* / さわらないで下さい). As is the case when shopping anywhere, if you break something, you are expected to pay for it.

Equally appealing is the restraint shown by vendors. As a general rule, vendors do not hawk their wares, fawn over the customer, or resort to high-pressure selling. To begin with, vendors do not try to attract attention to their merchandise. They sit behind their displays, waiting for customers to show up. When customers do show up, vendors do not usually approach or greet them. There is only rarely the welcoming "*irasshaimase*," so common in Japanese stores.

Another difference is the way prices are marked—or not marked, as is usually the case. Since final prices are decided by bargaining, most sellers like to have the flexibility to adjust asking prices on the spot (no one seems to consider the practice sneaky or underhanded). So when you ask how much something costs, sometimes it takes up to a minute to get an answer. You might hear the vendor say something like this:

> Well, let me see . . . This is an especially rare piece—I was really lucky to get this, you know—and, as you can see, it's in very good condition, especially considering its age. On the other hand, it is late in the day, and I haven't sold much today, so I suppose I should lower the price. And you look like a nice guy. So taking all that into consideration, I'm prepared to let this go for the very reasonable price of ¥7,500.

Of course, the vendor doesn't tell you that the price he decides partly reflects a perception of how badly you want to buy the item, not to mention his eagerness to sell. Some other factors determining an item's asking price (besides, of course, what the vendor paid for it) are whether other vendors are offering similar merchandise, and your skill at negotiating.

With the exception of very low-priced merchandise, it should go without saying that you are expected to talk down the price of anything you buy. Of course, there is nothing that says you have to. If you are content with the quoted figure, you are free to accept the vendor's initial asking price. Please be aware, however, that passively accepting the first price is tempting the vendor to overcharge the next foreign shopper. It is best not to set such a precedent.

While bargaining is the norm, bartering, swaps, or exchanges are virtually unheard of. Since vendors can buy things at auction for prices much lower than you can buy things at flea markets, it generally does not make economic sense for them to trade with you. Besides, vendors can always procure more stock. They prefer to move what they already have.

All merchandise is sold on a first-come, first-served basis—simply put, the first shopper to agree on a price with the vendor gets the goods. Merchandise is also sold on an as-is basis: when you agree to buy something, you agree to accept it in its present physical condition—dirty, damaged, or otherwise defective. No guarantee or warranty is ever offered.

Finally, merchandise is sold on a cash-only basis, and you are expected to pay on the spot. It is sometimes possible for a purchase to be held for a short time while you think it over or withdraw some cash. To have an item held you must pay a deposit in cash, and you will be asked to pay the balance in cash as well. Payment by credit card or check is not accepted.

Something which has already been sold or which has been held for another shopper will be set aside (where it is less likely to be noticed) and/or marked "sold"—in Japanese (*baiyaku-zumi*/売約済み or *go-yoyaku-zumi*/ご予約済み).

BARGAINING

The Negotiating Process

The process of bargaining or negotiating a price usually starts with the vendor establishing the asking price. The shopper then makes an offer, the vendor makes a counteroffer, and negotiations go back and forth until a price is agreed. As a general rule, the price agreed is about halfway between the vendor's asking price and the shopper's first offer.

The process becomes more interesting when the negotiations are interspersed with conversation. The shopper might find out how much something costs and then, without making an offer, ask how old it is and where it comes from. Later in the process the shopper might ask what the item was used for. Some shoppers prefer to get this kind of information before starting the bargaining process, so feel free to ask questions along the way. And don't be surprised if the vendor, being an easy-going type, takes you off on a tangent. After answering your questions he might tell you about the one owned by a friend and then suddenly ask where you are from.

Negotiations need not be rushed, and it is nicer —more in the spirit of flea-market shopping—if you do take your time. Meandering or staggered negotiations are pretty much the norm, and a style of negotiating that is too intense, focused, and business-like probably won't go down very well. You and the trader have time, so relax and enjoy it.

Sliding-Scale Discounts

With respect to discounts, the basic rule is the higher the asking price, the bigger the discount as a percentage of the asking price. Use the table below as a rough guide.

ASKING PRICE	DISCOUNT
Less than ¥1,000	0%
¥1,000–¥9,999	10%
¥10,000–¥24,999	15%
¥25,000–¥49,999	20%
¥50,000–¥99,999	25%
More than ¥100,000	30%

In order to negotiate a final price in line with the discount percentage shown, your initial offer needs to be considerably lower than that. For example, if the vendor asks for ¥20,000, you might offer ¥14,000, hoping that the vendor agrees to ¥17,000.

The price ranges in the Asking Price column are approximate, and percentage figures in the Discount column are typical or average.

Volume Discounts

Vendors are almost always willing to offer a larger discount if you buy more than one item. The idea is to give you a better deal for several items bundled together and sold for one all-inclusive price than for the same items sold separately. This is really just an extension of the sliding-scale discount principle, based on the logic that the vendor offers a bigger discount in percentage terms but earns a bigger profit in absolute terms. To work out approximately how big a discount to expect, simply add together the prices of the individual items and apply the same percentage.

It follows that you should negotiate a single price for everything you want to buy, rather than an individual price for each item. Be careful not to include any item that you are not completely sure you want, because if you decide at the last minute not to buy something, you will have to renegotiate the price of the whole lot.

Vendors sometimes try to tempt you to buy more by promising a larger-than-normal discount if you purchase in volume. To get you interested in additional items, they might suggest that

- you buy all the items in a set, not just one
- you buy something that goes with the item you are interested in
- you buy every item of its kind for sale ("Since you want these three, why don't you just buy all five of them?")
- you buy the entire box of stuff you are looking at
- you start a collection

This is about the closest thing to high-pressure selling that you will experience at a flea market. If you are uninterested, decline politely.

Items Thrown in for Free

If you are not sure you want to buy something, or if you are reluctant to accept the price you are being offered, a vendor might try to persuade you by throwing in something for free (*o-make*/お ま け). As often as not, the *o-make* item is something the vendor can easily do without, because it is worth little or has been hard to sell. Its value is seldom more than ten percent of the value of the main item.

You can look at the *o-make* item as a gift, as a reward for going through with the purchase, or as an additional discount, since it effectively lowers the price of the item you really want.

With skillful negotiation, you may be able to get the seller to throw in an item you select yourself. If the vendor is eager enough to make the sale, he/she might go for it in lieu of any additional price reduction.

Tips for Getting the Lowest Price

Negotiating may be an art, but any flea-market shopper can use the following tactics to increase the chances of getting the lowest possible price. Some of the most effective tactics are to:

- pretend to be less interested in the item than you really are
- examine the item carefully, making sure to point out any damage or defect
- suggest nicely that there is nothing special about the item compared to others like it
- act shocked by the asking price, and remain speechless (avoid making sarcastic comments)
- drag out the negotiating process by asking the vendor to tell you about the item you want to buy, or anything else you can think of to raise his/her hopes of making the sale—once you have the vendor emotionally involved, it is harder for him to let go of the sale, and the more likely he is to agree to your price
- negotiate a volume discount (see previous section)
- ask that an item be thrown in for free (see previous section)
- show up late in the day—traders prefer going home with less stuff than they brought

The vendor is probably a more skillful negotiator than you are, but by following these tips you can take away some of his advantage.

Unwritten Rules and Etiquette

Bargaining at flea markets takes place within a framework of unwritten rules and etiquette. The most important things to be aware of are mentioned in the list of DO's and DON'Ts that follows:

- DO remember to be polite and civil at all times; if you run across a rude or grumpy vendor, just walk away.
- DO keep your word once you agree to a price; DON'T back out of a purchase.
- DO keep more or less to the sliding-scale discount guidelines; DON'T make unreasonably low offers as it is insulting, and you might earn a reputation among vendors as a cheapskate.
- DON'T try to play vendors off against each other; trying to get one to meet or beat another's price is considered unnecessarily cut-throat and, at any rate, makes little sense because no two vendors sell merchandise that is identical.
- DON'T use sarcasm or flippancy as a negotiating tactic; it will probably not be understood or, worse yet, may be perceived as berating or bullying, whether or not it is intended as such.
- DON'T accuse a vendor of price gouging; if you suspect you are being swindled, terminate the negotiations by walking away.

Following these guidelines helps ensure a satisfying, stress-free, and successful flea-market shopping experience.

III. FLEA MARKET
   LISTINGS

This section contains a detailed list of 115 flea markets—indoor
and outdoor, large and small, famous and lesser known—held
throughout Japan.

The list includes about 80 to 85 percent of the flea markets selling
Japanese antiques, which makes it the most comprehensive ever com-
piled. It does not include all the flea markets in Japan. Excluded are
flea markets selling only or primarily everyday items such as food,
personal-care products, shoes, and clothing as well as those selling
only or primarily Western antiques or toys. Flea markets selling Japanese antiques were excluded only if their organizers could not be
reached to verify information or if they attract less than ten vendors.

The listings are divided into three sections—Tokyo and the Kantō
Area, Kyoto/Osaka and the Kansai Area, and Other Regions. In the
first section, there is a subdivision for Tokyo (the 23 city wards as
well as outlying areas within metropolitan Tokyo) and one for each of
the surrounding prefectures (Kanagawa, Chiba, Saitama, Tochigi, Ibaraki, and Gunma). The second section lists flea markets by city (Kyoto,
Osaka, Kobe, and Nara) and one prefecture, Shiga, while in the third
section flea markets are listed by region, from north to south, starting
with Hokkaidō and ending with Kyūshū.

The official name of each flea market is given in both Romanized

Japanese and standard Japanese characters; this is mostly for reference, since many names are not well known or often used, even among vendors.

Monthly flea markets tend to be held outdoors on the grounds of a temple or shrine, while flea markets taking place intermittently (a certain number of times per year) tend to be held indoors at special venues (typically, an exhibition center, warehouse, or public hall).

As a general rule, indoor markets tend to be better organized, to be attended by more vendors, and to attract more shoppers. Since there are more potential customers, vendors tend to bring a wider assortment of merchandise and to make a greater effort to display their wares in an attractive and appealing way.

Timing and Weather

Most flea markets take place on a regular monthly schedule—either on the same day (or days) or the same date (or dates). However, there are often deviations from the regular schedule, planned and announced in advance. Most deviations from schedule are due to a national holiday, a festival, a day of special religious observance, or other special events.

A small number of flea markets are held between one and five times per year. These usually last two or three days, and once the date is set, there are no changes. Owing to the need to book space in advance and other logistical considerations, the exact dates are not decided until a few months before the market takes place (and will vary from year to year), so it is necessary to contact the organizer *in Japanese* to get the information.

It is important to realize that a flea market's publicly announced or official start and finish times more often than not differ from its actual start and finish times. There are two basic reasons for this. First, for purposes of scheduling, the definitions of "sunrise" and "sunset" are quite loose; vendors often show up after sunrise or leave before sunset.

Second, traders almost invariably start to pack up their merchandise one to two hours before the scheduled finish time. Having begun preparations for departure, some are happy to interrupt what they are doing to interact with shoppers and try to make a last-minute sale. Others are not, and make it clear that they are effectively closed. (With respect to flea markets lasting two or more days, this point applies only to the final day.)

Fluctuations in the weather can and often do impact outdoor flea markets, but policy varies from market to market. In the event of rain or snow, the flea market may continue, be canceled, or be canceled only if it is raining hard. As the determination of what constitutes a "raining hard" is up to the organizers, it is best to call on the morning of the flea market to find out if the event is still on. If you are unable to reach someone, it is probably best to stay home on a rainy, snowy, or stormy day, since the organizers tend to play it safe.

Getting There

Taking the train and/or subway is generally the easiest and fastest way to get to a flea market, especially in urban areas. The list shows which train(s) or subway line(s) to take and the closest or most convenient station(s). In many cases it is possible to get to the flea market on more than one line or from more than one station. For some venues, there may be access routes not shown; those shown are recommended by the organizers.

The approximate number of minutes to walk from station to market is indicated in parentheses. If it is too far to walk, the information for bus or car/taxi is given. The organizers of some indoor flea markets arrange for free shuttle-bus service from the closest major train station to the venue.

"Getting There" gives easy-to-follow directions to the venue from the closest or most convenient station. To obtain a map showing how to get to the venue, contact the organizers, who often can fax, mail, or e-mail one (although it is likely to be in Japanese).

For those going by car or motorbike, keep in mind that parking is generally available only at indoor markets.

Other Information

The approximate number of vendors, rounded to the nearest multiple of five, is given as an indication of the size of the flea market. Some of the vendors counted in this number may sell Western antiques or everyday items.

Knowing the year the market was established is useful because, all other things being equal, the longer a flea market has been running, the better it is known and the more vendors and shoppers it attracts.

The phone numbers are for the organizers unless otherwise indicated. In nearly every case, Japanese is required. For some flea markets, both a cell-phone number (with prefixes 090 or 070) and a regular phone number are provided. As a general rule, use the cell-phone number to contact the organizers on the day of the flea market and the regular phone number at other times. Sometimes the telephone numbers of the venues (a temple, shrine, or hall) are included as a back-up number, but these should only be used as a last resort.

Accuracy of Information

The information contained in the listings was accurate and up-to-date at the time this book went to press. If you become aware of any new markets or errors, kindly send an e-mail message to the author at <theo_manning@hotmail.com> or to the publisher.

TOKYO AND THE KANTŌ AREA

TOKYO

Central Tokyo (23 Wards)

1. **Nogi Jinja Komingu Kottō Ichi** 乃木神社 古民具骨董市

LOCATION: Nogizaka, Nogi Shrine (乃木神社)
NEAREST STATION: Nogizaka (乃木坂) (1 min.), Chiyoda subway line
WHEN: 2nd Sunday (except November), 7:00 A.M.–3:00 P.M.
RAINY WEATHER: Canceled　VENDORS: 35–40　ESTABLISHED: 1977
GETTING THERE: As you come out Exit 1, turn left. The entrance to the shrine is about 10 meters ahead on the left.
ADDRESS: Nogi Shrine, 8–11–27 Akasaka, Minato-ku
　　　　港区赤坂8–11–27　乃木神社
CONTACT: 0426–91–3572, 03–3478–3001 (Nogi Shrine)

2. **Roppongi Antique Fair** 六本木アンティックフェア

LOCATION: Roppongi, Roi Building (ロアビル)
NEAREST STATION: Roppongi (六本木) (4 min.), Hibiya subway line
WHEN: 4th Thursday, 4th Friday, 8:00 A.M.–evening
RAINY WEATHER: Okay　VENDORS: 20　ESTABLISHED: 1976
GETTING THERE: Come out Exit 3, turn right. Cross the narrow street just beyond the Almond sweet shop and you are at the major intersection known as Roppongi

Crossing. Turn right, and walk about 250 meters down Gaien Higashi Dōri (toward Tokyo Tower). The Roi Building is 200 meters down on the right (the corner with the signal). The vendors are gathered in front of the building, on the steps.

ADDRESS: Roi Building, 5–5–1 Roppongi, Minato-ku

港区六本木5-5-1　ロアビル

CONTACT: 03–3583–2081

3. **Tōgō no Mori Nomi no Ichi**　東郷の杜 能美の市

LOCATION: Harajuku, Tōgō Shrine (東郷神社)

NEAREST STATION: Meiji Jingū-mae (明治神宮前) (5 min.), Chiyoda subway line
• Harajuku (原宿) (10 min.), JR Yamanote Line

WHEN: 1st Sunday, 4th Sunday, 4:00 A.M.–3:00 P.M.

RAINY WEATHER: Canceled

VENDORS: 130–150　**ESTABLISHED:** 1978

GETTING THERE: From Meiji Jingū-mae Station: Take Exit 5. Walk downhill to the first intersection. Turn left and walk about 250 meters, passing through an intersection with a traffic light. The entrance to the shrine is on the left, just before the second light.

From Harajuku Station: Cross the street, turn right, and make your way to the top of Aoyama Dōri, the wide tree-lined boulevard. Walk about 200 meters downhill, until you see the entrance to Meiji Jingū-mae Station, and from there, follow the directions above.

ADDRESS: Tōgō Shrine, 1–5–3 Jingū-mae, Shibuya-ku

渋谷区神宮前1-5-3　東郷神社

CONTACT: 03–3425–7965, 03–3403–3591 (Tōgō Shrine)

4. **Hanazono Jinja Aozora Kottō Ichi**　花園神社青空骨董市

LOCATION: Shinjuku, Hanazono Shrine (花園神社)

NEAREST STATION: Shinjuku 3-chōme (新宿三丁目) (5 min.), Marunouchi/
Toei Shinjuku subway lines • Shinjuku (新宿) (10 min.), JR Yamanote/Chūō/
Sōbu/Saikyō lines

WHEN: Every Sunday, sunrise–sunset

RAINY WEATHER: Canceled　**VENDORS:** 100　**ESTABLISHED:** 1980

GETTING THERE: From Shinjuku 3-chōme Station: As you come out Exit B3, turn left. Walk about 200 meters, passing through two traffic lights, then look for the entrance to the grounds of the shrine on your left. From Shinjuku Station: Come out the East Exit, and look for the big screen (Studio Alta) on the building across the street. Cross the street and turn right. Walk along this street for about 300 meters until you reach the fourth traffic light. Turn left at the light (Isetan department store is on the corner). Walk about 30 meters, or until you see Exit B3 of Shinjuku 3-chōme Station on the left. From there, follow the directions above.

ADDRESS: Hanazono Shrine, 5–17–3 Shinjuku, Shinjuku-ku
新宿区新宿5-17-3 花園神社
CONTACT: 03–3200–3093 (Hanazono Shrine)

5. Kishibojin Kottō Ichi   鬼子母神 骨董市

LOCATION: Toshima-ku, Kishibojin Shrine (鬼子母神)
NEAREST STATION: Kishibojin-mae (鬼子母神前) (5 min.), Toden Arakawa
Line • *Additional Station:* Ikebukuro (池袋), JR Yamanote/Saikyō lines
WHEN: 4th Saturday, 7:00 A.M.–sunset
RAINY WEATHER: Canceled   VENDORS: 20–30   ESTABLISHED: 2000
GETTING THERE: From Kishibojin-mae Station: As you exit the station, head in
the direction of Kishibojin, which is to the northwest. Follow the main street for
about 250 meters, keeping to the left where the road forks. The shrine is on the
right. From Ikebukuro Station about 7 minutes by car/taxi.
ADDRESS: Kishibojin Shrine, 3–15–20 Zōshigaya, Toshima-ku
豊島区雑司が谷3-15-20 鬼子母神
CONTACT: 0475–55–8505, 090–8771–9850, 03–3982–8347 (Kishibojin Shrine)

6. Iidabashi Ramura Kottō Antique Aozora Ichi
飯田橋ラムラ・骨董アンティック青空市

LOCATION: Iidabashi, Central Plaza (セントラルプラザ)
NEAREST STATION: Iidabashi (飯田橋) (1 min.), JR Sōbu Line, Tōzai/Yurakuchō/
Nanboku subway lines
WHEN: 1st Saturday, 6:00 A.M.–sunset
RAINY WEATHER: Okay   VENDORS: 40–50   ESTABLISHED: 1987
GETTING THERE: Central Plaza is a sort of courtyard within the Iidabashi train-
and subway-station complex. Follow the signs.
ADDRESS: Central Plaza, 1–1 Kaguragashi, Shinjuku-ku
新宿区神楽河岸1-1 セントラルプラザ
CONTACT: 03–3917–5426 (taped information), 03–3260–8211 (Central Plaza)

7. Tokyo Dome Prism Kottō Fair
東京ドーム プリズム骨董フェア

LOCATION: Kōrakuen, Tokyo Dome Prism Hall (東京ドーム, プリズムホール)
NEAREST STATION: Suidōbashi (水道橋) (5 min.), JR Sōbu/Toei Mita subway
lines • Kōrakuen (後楽園) (3 min.), Marunouchi/Nanboku subway lines
WHEN: May (3 days), November (3 days), 10:00 A.M.–5:00 P.M. (last day 10:00 A.M.–
4:00 P.M.)
RAINY WEATHER: Held indoors   VENDORS: 150   ESTABLISHED: 1995
ENTRANCE FEE: ¥1,000 (¥800 in advance)

GETTING THERE: From Suidōbashi Station: Take the West Exit, turn right, walk about 20 meters, and take the catwalk that crosses a river and a major street. The Tokyo Dome complex is on the other side. Once inside the complex, follow the signs to Prism Hall, the exhibition space where the flea market is held.

From Kōrakuen Station: Take Exit 2 or Exit 3 and, heading towards the base-ball stadium, take the catwalk that crosses a major street. Continue in the same direction until you find your way into the Tokyo Dome complex. Once inside, follow the signs to Prism Hall.

ADDRESS: Prism Hall, Tokyo Dome, 1–3–61 Kōraku, Bunkyō-ku

文京区後楽1-3-61　東京ドーム, プリズムホール

CONTACT: 0276–38–3417, 090–3348–7760, 03–3817–6222 (Tokyo Dome, Prism Hall)

8. Ueno Kōen Aki no Kottō Matsuri　上野公園 秋の骨董祭り

LOCATION: Ueno, Ueno Park, Shinobazu Pond (上野公園不忍池)
NEAREST STATION: Ueno (上野) (2 min.) JR Yamanote/Keihin Tōhoku lines
WHEN: October 1–31, daily, 8:00 A.M.–sunset
RAINY WEATHER: Okay　**VENDORS:** 40–60　**ESTABLISHED:** 2000
GETTING THERE: As you come out the Shinobazu Exit, turn left. Walk about 350 meters, following the curved road in a clockwise direction along the edge of the park/pond, until you see the flea market.
ADDRESS: Shinobazu Pond, 2–1 Ueno Kōen (Park), Taito-ku

台東区上野公園2-1　不忍池

CONTACT: 03–3917–5426

9. Ueno Natsu Matsuri Yoru no Kottō Ichi
上野夏祭り 夜の骨董市

LOCATION: Ueno, Ueno Park, Shinobazu Pond (上野公園不忍池)
NEAREST STATION: Ueno (上野) (2 min.) JR Yamanote/Keihin Tōhoku lines
WHEN: July 17–August 10, daily, 4:00 P.M.–10:00 P.M.
RAINY WEATHER: Okay　**VENDORS:** 50　**ESTABLISHED:** 1982
GETTING THERE: As you come out the Shinobazu Exit, turn left. Walk about 350 meters, following the curved road in a clockwise direction along the edge of the park/pond, until you see the flea market.
ADDRESS: Shinobazu Pond, 2–1 Ueno Kōen (Park), Taito-ku

台東区上野公園2-1　不忍池

CONTACT: 03–3917–5426

10. Yasukuni Jinja Aozora Kottō Ichi　靖国神社 青空骨董市

LOCATION: Chiyoda-ku, Yasukuni Shrine (靖国神社)

NEAREST STATION: Kudanshita (九段下) (5 min.), Hanzōmon/Tōzai/Toei Shinjuku subway lines

WHEN: 3rd Sunday (in July, either 2nd Sunday or 3rd Sunday preempted by festival; contact organizer for details), sunrise–sunset

RAINY WEATHER: Light rain, okay   VENDORS: 40   ESTABLISHED: 1996

GETTING THERE: Take Exit 1, then follow Yasukuni Dōri uphill for about 100 meters, keeping the Budōkan on your left. The entrance to the grounds of the shrine is on the right.

ADDRESS: Yasukuni Shrine, 3–1–1 Kudan Kita, Chiyoda-ku

千代田区九段北3-1-1　靖国神社

CONTACT: 090–2723–0687, 03–3261–8326 (Yasukuni Shrine)

11. Heiwajima Zenkoku Komingu Kottō Matsuri
平和島 全国古民具骨董祭り

LOCATION: Ōta-ku, Heiwajima, Tokyo Ryūtsū Center (東京流通センター)

NEAREST STATION: Ryūtsū Center (流通センター) (1 min.), Tokyo Monorail (accessible via Hamamatsuchō Station on JR Yamanote/Keihin Tōhoku lines)

WHEN: February or March (3 days), May (3 days), June (3 days), September (3 days), December (3 days), 10:00 A.M.–6:00 P.M. (last day 10:00 A.M.–5:00 P.M.)

RAINY WEATHER: Held indoors

VENDORS: 250   ESTABLISHED: 1977

GETTING THERE: Come out the exit, and look across the street, slightly to your left. You'll see the Tokyo Ryūtsū Center, a warehouse-like building with a small plaza in front. Enter the building and follow the signs to the exhibition hall where the flea market is held.

ADDRESS: Tokyo Ryūtsū Center, 6–1–1 Heiwajima, Ōta-ku

大田区平和島6-1-1　東京流通センター

CONTACT: 03–3980–8228, 03–3767–2111 (Tokyo Ryūtsū Center)

12. Kottō & Antique Tenji Sokubaikai
骨董＆アンティック展示即売会

LOCATION: Hamamatsuchō, Toritsu Sangyō Bōeki Center (都立産業貿易センター)

NEAREST STATION: Hamamatsuchō (浜松町) (5 min.), JR Yamanote/Keihin Tōhoku lines

WHEN: Spring (3 days), fall (3 days), 10:00 A.M.–5:00 P.M. (last day 10:00 A.M.–4:00 P.M.)

RAINY WEATHER: Held indoors   VENDORS: 50   ESTABLISHED: 2001

GETTING THERE: Come out the North Exit, turn right (to the east) onto the main street. Walk past the expressway and go another 100 meters. The Toritsu Sangyō Bōeki Center is on the right.

ADDRESS: Toritsu Sangyō Bōeki Center, 1–7–8 Kaigan, Minato-ku
港区海岸1–7–8　都立産業貿易センター（浜松町館）
CONTACT: 046–281–6171, 03–3434–4241 (Toritsu Sangyō Bōeki Center)

13. **Kottō Jamboree**　骨董ジャンボリー

LOCATION: Odaiba, Tokyo Big Sight (Tokyo International Exhibition Center)
（東京ビッグサイト［東京国際展示場］）
NEAREST STATION: Kokusai Tenjijō Seimon-mae (国際展示場正門前) (3 min.),
Yurikamome Line (accessible via Shinbashi Station on JR Yamanote/Keihin
Tōhoku/Tōkaidō/Yokosuka lines)
WHEN: Summer (3 days), winter (3 days), 10:00 A.M.–5:00 P.M.
RAINY WEATHER: Held indoors　**VENDORS:** 500　**ESTABLISHED:** 1997
ENTRANCE FEE: First day, ¥3,000 (¥2,000 in advance); second/third days, ¥1,000
(¥800)
GETTING THERE: Take the South Exit. Follow the signs from the station to the
exhibition center. There are several exhibition halls, but the one where the flea
market is held should be clearly marked.
ADDRESS: Tokyo Big Sight, 3–21–1 Ariake, Kōtō-ku
江東区有明3–21–1　東京ビッグサイト
CONTACT: 03–5996–4105, 03–5536–1111 (Tokyo Big Sight)

14. **Tomioka Hachimangū Kottō Ichi**　富岡八幡宮 骨董市

LOCATION: Kōtō-ku, Tomioka Hachimangū Shrine (富岡八幡宮)
NEAREST STATION: Monzen Nakachō (門前仲町) (3 min.), Tōzai subway line
WHEN: 1st Sunday (mostly Western antiques), 2nd Sunday (in January, 2nd Sun-
day only), 6:00 A.M.–5:00 P.M.
RAINY WEATHER: Light rain, okay　**VENDORS:** 100　**ESTABLISHED:** 1994
GETTING THERE: As you come out Exit 1, turn left. Follow this street for about 100
meters. Take the second left. The grounds of the shrine are about 100 meters ahead,
directly in front of you.
ADDRESS: Tomioka Hachimangū Shrine, 1–20–3 Tomioka, Kōtō-ku
江東区富岡1–20–3　富岡八幡宮
CONTACT: 0276–38–3417, 03–3642–1315 (Tomioka Hachimangū)

15. **Arai Yakushi Kottō Ichi**　新井薬師 骨董市

LOCATION: Nakano-ku, Arai Yakushi Temple (新井薬師)
NEAREST STATION: Arai Yakushi-mae (新井薬師前) (5 min.), Seibu Shinjuku Line
WHEN: 1st Sunday (in January, 2nd Sunday), sunrise–sunset
RAINY WEATHER: Light rain, okay
VENDORS: 80　**ESTABLISHED:** 1977

GETTING THERE: After coming out the South Exit, find the major street that crosses the train tracks, about 20 meters to the right. Heading away from the tracks, follow this street for about 150 meters, until you get to a traffic light. At the light, take a half-right. The entrance to the temple is about 200 meters ahead on the right.

ADDRESS: Arai Yakushi Temple, 5–3–5 Arai, Nakano-ku

中野区新井5-3-5　新井薬師

CONTACT: 03–3319–6033

16. **Hikawa Jinja Kottō Ichi**　氷川神社 骨董市

LOCATION: Nerima-ku, Hikawa Shrine (氷川神社)

NEAREST STATION: Shakujii Kōen (石神井公園), Seibu Ikebukuro Line

WHEN: 4th Sunday, sunrise–4:00 P.M.

RAINY WEATHER: Canceled

VENDORS: 20–30　**ESTABLISHED:** 1998

GETTING THERE: From Shakujii Kōen Station about 7 minutes by car/taxi. Or use the bus from South Exit of the station for Ogikubo (荻窪). Get off at JA Tokyo Aoba-mae (JA東京あおば前), walk back along the bus route for about 2 minutes to Shakujii Shō crossing (with an elementary school on the corner), then turn left. Walk for another 2 minutes to the first signal, take the right fork, and turn right at the first corner. The shrine is at the end of the road.

ADDRESS: Hikawa Shrine, 1–18–24 Shakujii-dai, Nerima-ku

練馬区石神井台1-18-24　氷川神社

CONTACT: 03–3319–6033, 03–3997–6032 (Hikawa Shrine)

17. **Ōmiya Hachimangū Komingu Kottō Ichi**
大宮八幡宮 古民具骨董市

LOCATION: Suginami-ku, Ōmiya Hachimangū Shrine (大宮八幡宮)

NEAREST STATION: Nishi-Eifuku (西永福) (8 min.), Keiō Inokashira Line

WHEN: 4th Saturday and Sunday, sunrise–sunset

RAINY WEATHER: Light rain, okay

VENDORS: 20　**ESTABLISHED:** 1996

GETTING THERE: As you come out the exit, turn left, and immediately left again. Cross over the train tracks, then continue walking for about 150 meters, until you reach a T-junction. Turn left at the T-junction, then go about 100 meters, until you get to a traffic light. Turn right at the light. Walk about 400 meters, to the second light, and turn left. The entrance to the grounds of the shrine is about 100 meters ahead on the left.

ADDRESS: Ōmiya Hachimangū Shrine, 2–3–1 Ōmiya, Suginami-ku

杉並区大宮2-3-1　大宮八幡宮

CONTACT: 03–3302–4545, 090–2230–4545, 03–3311–0105 (Ōmiya Hachimangū Shrine)

18. Setagaya Boro Ichi 世田谷ボロ市

LOCATION: Setagaya-ku, Boro Ichi Dōri (street) (ボロ市通り)
NEAREST STATION: Setagaya (世田谷) (12 min.), Tōkyū Setagaya Line
WHEN: December 15 and 16, January 15 and 16, 9:00 A.M.–9:00 P.M.
RAINY WEATHER: Okay
VENDORS: 700 (more than half of the vendors sell everyday merchandise)
GETTING THERE: As you come out the exit, turn left. Walk about 100 meters, until you reach a T-junction with a traffic light. Turn left at the T-junction. Turn right at the next light. Walk another 150 meters to the next light, and turn right. This is Boro Ichi street, where the flea market takes place.
ADDRESS: Boro Ichi Dōri, 1-chōme Setagaya, Setagaya-ku
　　　　　世田谷区世田谷1丁目ボロ市通り
CONTACT: 03–5432–1111 (ward office)

19. Shinmeigū Garakuta Ichi 神明宮がらくた市

LOCATION: Suginami-ku, Shinmeigū Shrine (神明宮)
NEAREST STATION: Asagaya (阿佐ヶ谷) (2 min.), JR Chūō/Sōbu lines
WHEN: 1st Saturday, 6:00 A.M.–4:00 P.M.
RAINY WEATHER: Light rain, okay　**ESTABLISHED:** 1997
VENDORS: 40
GETTING THERE: Take the North Exit. Follow the narrow street that leads diagonally off to the right for about 200 meters, staying to the left where it forks, until it reaches a T-junction. The grounds of the shrine are directly in front of you.
ADDRESS: Shinmeigū Shrine, 1–25–5 Asagaya Kita, Suginami-ku
　　　　　杉並区阿佐谷北1–25–5　神明宮
CONTACT: 03–3395–2262, 090–3216–1973, 03–3330–4824 (Shinmeigū Shrine)

Outlying Tokyo

20. Higashi Fushimi Eki-mae Kottō Ichi 東伏見駅前骨董市

LOCATION: Nishi Tokyo-shi, in front of Higashi Fushimi Station (東伏見駅前)
NEAREST STATION: Higashi Fushimi (東伏見) (1 min.), Seibu Shinjuku Line
WHEN: 2nd Saturday (April–December), 2nd Monday (January–March), 6:00 A.M.–4:00 P.M.
RAINY WEATHER: Light rain, okay　**VENDORS:** 50　**ESTABLISHED:** 2001
GETTING THERE: The flea market is held in the open area of the Ice Arena in front of the South Exit. Go out this exit, and you can't miss it.
ADDRESS: Higashi Fushimi 3–1–25, Nishi Tokyo-shi
　　　　　西東京市東伏見3–1–25　東伏見駅前
CONTACT: 03–5996–4105, 090–1811–0220

21. **Tanashi Jinja Aozora Kottō Ichi**
田無神社 青空骨董市

LOCATION: Nishi Tokyo-shi, Tanashi Shrine (田無神社)

NEAREST STATION: Tanashi (田無) (5 min.), Seibu Shinjuku Line

WHEN: 1st Saturday, sunrise–sunset

RAINY WEATHER: Light rain, okay

VENDORS: 40   ESTABLISHED: 1998

GETTING THERE: Come out the North Exit, walk north for 200 meters to Ōme Kaidō, then turn right. The shrine is 300 meters down on the far left.

ADDRESS: Tanashi Shrine, 3–7–4 Tanashi-machi, Nishi Tokyo-shi
西東京市田無町3–7–4　田無神社

CONTACT: 090–2723–0687, 0424–61–4442 (Tanashi Shrine)

22. **Chōfu Tenjin Ichi** 調布天神市

LOCATION: Chōfu-shi, Fuda Tenjin Shrine (布多天神)

NEAREST STATION: Chōfu (調布) (8 min.), Keio Line

WHEN: 25th of month, 9:00 A.M.–5:00 P.M.

RAINY WEATHER: Okay   VENDORS: 15

GETTING THERE: Take the North Exit. Follow the major shopping street running perpendicular to the train tracks for about 250 meters, until you reach a T-junction. Turn right at the T-junction, then take the first left. Go straight for about 100 meters, until you see the grounds of the shrine directly ahead.

ADDRESS: Fuda Tenjin Shrine, 1–8–1 Chōfugaoka, Chōfu-shi
調布市調布ヶ丘1–8–1　布多天神

CONTACT: 0424–89–0022 (Fuda Tenjin Shrine)

23. **Takahata Fudō Gozare Ichi** 高幡不動ござれ市

LOCATION: Hino-shi, Takahata Fudō Temple (高幡不動)

NEAREST STATION: Takahata Fudō (高幡不動) (2 min.), Keiō Line

WHEN: 3rd Sunday, 8:00 A.M.–4:00 P.M.

RAINY WEATHER: Okay

VENDORS: 80   ESTABLISHED: 1988

GETTING THERE: As you come out the exit, turn right. Walk along the shopping street running parallel to the train tracks for about 150 meters, until it ends in a T-junction. Turn left at the T-junction. The entrance to the grounds of the temple is about 20 meters ahead on the right.

ADDRESS: Takahata Fudō Temple, 733 Takahata, Hino-shi
日野市高幡733　高幡不動

CONTACT: 0428–86–2950, 090–3314–1994, 042–591–0032 (Takahata Fudō Temple)

24. Hachiōji Sengen Jinja Silk Road Mukashi Ichi
八王子浅間神社シルクロード昔市

LOCATION: Hachiōji-shi, Sengen Shrine (浅間神社)

NEAREST STATION: Yamada (山田) (8 min.), Keio Takao Line • Hachiōji, JR Chūō Line

WHEN: 4th Sunday, 10:00 A.M.–5:00 P.M.

RAINY WEATHER: Light rain, okay

VENDORS: 40   ESTABLISHED: 1999

GETTING THERE: From Yamada Station: Walk north about 1 kilometer to the shrine. From Hachiōji Station: Take a bus from the North Exit and get off at Shimin-Taiikukan-mae (市民体育館前) bus stop (about 13 minutes).

ADDRESS: Sengen Shrine, Fujimori Kōen (Park), 2–2–3 Dai-machi, Hachiōji-shi
八王子市台町2–2–3（富士森公園内）浅間神社

CONTACT: 0426–28–2933

25. Akishima Kottō Antique Fair
昭島 骨董アンティックフェア

LOCATION: Akishima-shi, Messe Akishima (メッセ昭島)

NEAREST STATION: Akishima (昭島) (5 min.), JR Ōme Line

WHEN: May (3 days), November (3 days), 10:00 A.M.–5:00 P.M.

RAINY WEATHER: Held indoors   VENDORS: 160   ESTABLISHED: 1991

GETTING THERE: Take the North Exit. Walk about 100 meters until you hit a T-junction. Turn right at the T-junction. Go to the second light and turn left. Messe Akishima is about 250 meters ahead on the right.

ADDRESS: Messe Akishima, 2–8–55 Tsutsujigaoka, Akishima-shi
昭島市つつじヶ丘2–8–55　メッセ昭島

CONTACT: 042–546–5171, 090–1116–2282, 042–543–6118 (Messe Akishima)

26. Fussa Shichi Fukujin Takara Ichi   福生七福神 宝市

LOCATION: Fussa-shi, Kumakawa Shrine (熊川神社)

NEAREST STATION: Haijima (拝島) (15 min.), JR Ōme/Hachikō lines, Seibu Haijima Line

WHEN: 2nd Sunday, sunrise–4:00 P.M.

RAINY WEATHER: Light rain, okay

VENDORS: 45   ESTABLISHED: 1989

GETTING THERE: Come out the South Exit and walk west for about 700 meters. Turn left at Uchide Crossing (Idemitsu Gas Station). The shrine is about 30 meters down the road on the left, behind Denny's.

ADDRESS: Kumakawa Shrine, 659 Kumakawa, Fussa-shi
福生市熊川659　熊川神社

CONTACT: 03–3395–2262, 090–3216–1973, 042–551–0720 (Kumakawa Shrine)

27. **Machida Tenmangū Garakuta Kottō Ichi**
町田天満宮がらくた骨董市

LOCATION: Machida-shi, Machida Tenmangū Shrine (町田天満宮)
NEAREST STATION: Machida (町田) (8 min.), JR Yokohama and Odakyū lines
WHEN: 1st of month (in January, held on the 8th), 8:00 A.M.–4:00 P.M.
RAINY WEATHER: Light rain, okay   VENDORS: 80   ESTABLISHED: 1994
GETTING THERE: Come out the Tōkyū Hands Exit, and follow the posted flags or
banners. The flea market is near the tracks. 300 meters southeast of the station.
ADDRESS: Machida Tenmangū Shrine, 1–21–5 Haramachida, Machida-shi
　　　　町田市原町田1–21–5　町田天満宮
CONTACT: 042–886–2950, 042–722–2325 (Machida Tenmangū Shrine)

OUTLYING AREAS

Kanagawa

28. **Kottō Antique Fair**　骨董アンティックフェア

LOCATION: Yokohama, Yokohama Arena (横浜アリーナ)
NEAREST STATION: Shin-Yokohama (新横浜) (5 min.), JR Yokohama/Tōkaidō
Shinkansen lines
WHEN: February (2 days), September (2 days), 11:00 A.M.–5:00 P.M.
RAINY WEATHER: Held indoors   VENDORS: 120   ESTABLISHED: 1998
GETTING THERE: As you come out Exit 6, turn left. Walk along this street for about
400 meters. The arena is on the left, just after the third side street on the left.
ADDRESS: Yokohama Arena, 3–10 Shin-Yokohama, Kita-ku, Yokohama-shi, Kana-
gawa　神奈川県横浜市北区新横浜3–10　横浜アリーナ
CONTACT: 042–546–5171, 090–1116–2282, 045–474–4000 (Yokohama Arena)

29. **Yokohama Kottō Ichi**　ザ 横浜骨董市

LOCATION: Yokohama, Sanbō Hall (横浜産貿ホール)
NEAREST STATION: Kannai (関内) (12 min.), JR Negishi/Yokohama lines, Yoko-
hama subway line
WHEN: Spring, fall; call for specific dates, 10:00 A.M.–6:00 P.M. (last day 10:00 A.M.–
4:00 P.M.)
RAINY WEATHER: Held indoors   VENDORS: 30   ESTABLISHED: 1991
GETTING THERE: As you come out the South Exit, turn right. Follow the street that
runs parallel to the train tracks for about 250 meters until you get to Yokohama
Stadium. Just beyond the stadium, turn left onto a major street. Follow this street

for about 500 meters, all the way to the harbor. Turn right just after a large gray concrete building known as the Silk Center. Sanbō Hall is about 100 meters ahead on the right, just as the harborside park comes into view.

ADDRESS: Yokohama Sanbō Hall, 2 Yamashita-chō, Naka-ku, Yokohama-shi, Kanagawa　神奈川県横浜市中区山下町2　横浜産貿ホール

CONTACT: 046–281–6171, 045–671–7050 (Yokohama Sanbō Hall)

30. **Yokohama Kottō World**　横浜骨董ワールド

LOCATION: Yokohama, Pacifico Yokohama (パシフィコ横浜)

NEAREST STATION: Sakuragichō (桜木町) (7 min.), JR Negishi/Yokohama lines, Tōkyū Tōyoko Line

WHEN: March (3 days), November (3 days), 10:00 A.M.–5:00 P.M. (first day, noon–5:00 P.M.)

RAINY WEATHER: Held indoors

VENDORS: 350   **ESTABLISHED:** 2002

ENTRANCE FEE: ¥1,000 (¥800 in advance)

GETTING THERE: Go through the ticket turnstile, turn left, and make your way out of the station. Veer to the left, go up the escalator, and take the "moving sidewalk" that transports people to the base of Landmark Tower. Get off at about the halfway point, and take the stairs back down to street level. Heading further away from the station, walk about 500 meters along the street passing in front of Landmark Plaza and Queen's Square shopping centers. Hotel Pacifico Yokohama is on your left.

ADDRESS: Pacifico Yokohama, 1–1–1 Minato Mirai, Nishi-ku, Yokohama-shi, Kanagawa　神奈川県横浜市西区みなとみらい1–1–1　パシフィコ横浜

CONTACT: 0428–86–2950, 045–221–2155 (Pacifico Yokohama)

31. **Tatsu no Kuchi Dai Kottō Ichi**　龍の口 大骨董市

LOCATION: Kanagawa-ken, Enoshima, Ryūkōji Temple (龍口寺)

NEAREST STATION: Enoshima (江ノ島) (3 min.), Enoden Line • *Additional station:* Katase Enoshima (片瀬江ノ島) (10 min.), Odakyū Enoshima Line

WHEN: 3rd Sunday, sunrise–sunset

RAINY WEATHER: Okay (held indoors in event of rain)

VENDORS: 80–100   **ESTABLISHED:** 1998

GETTING THERE: From Enoshima Station: Exit the station, then head north for about 50 meters on the street that crosses the train tracks, until you reach a traffic light. Turn right at the light. The entrance to the grounds of the temple is about 200 meters ahead on the left.

ADDRESS: Ryūkōji Temple, 3–13–37 Katase, Fujisawa-shi, Kanagawa
神奈川県藤沢市片瀬3–13–37　龍口寺

CONTACT: 0466–25–7222 (Ryūkōji Temple)

32. Shōnan Kottō Nomi no Ichi
湘南 骨董蚤の市

LOCATION: Kanagawa-ken, Fujisawa, Yugyōji Temple (遊行寺)
NEAREST STATION: Fujisawa (藤沢), JR Tōkaidō/Odakyū Enoshima lines
WHEN: 1st Sunday, 4th Sunday, 8:00 A.M.–4:00 P.M.
RAINY WEATHER: Okay
VENDORS: 50   **ESTABLISHED:** 1985
GETTING THERE: From the station the temple is a 6-minute car/taxi ride. Or board a bus for Totsuka (戸塚) and get off at the Yugyōji-mae (遊行寺前) bus stop. On foot, the temple is a 15-minute walk to the north from the station.
ADDRESS: Yugyōji Temple, 1–8–1 Nishitomi, Fujisawa-shi, Kanagawa
神奈川県藤沢市西富1–8–1　遊行寺
CONTACT: 046–535–2766, 0466–22–2063 (Yugyōji Temple)

33. Hōshu no Ichi   宝珠の市

LOCATION: Kanagawa-ken, Tsujidō, Hōshuji Temple (宝珠寺)
NEAREST STATION: Tsujidō (辻堂) (9 min.), JR Tōkaidō Line
WHEN: 5th of month, 8:00 A.M.–3:00 P.M.
RAINY WEATHER: Light rain, okay
VENDORS: 50   **ESTABLISHED:** 1998
GETTING THERE: Take the North Exit and walk east along the tracks for about 1 kilometer. Turn right at the Eneos Gas Station. Go another 150 meters and turn right. The temple is on the right.
ADDRESS: Hōshuji Temple, 2–4–27 Tsujido Motomachi, Fujisawa-shi, Kanagawa
神奈川県藤沢市辻堂元町2–4–27　宝珠寺
CONTACT: 0466–34–0819, 090–3314–1994, 0466–36–8427 (Hōshuji Temple)

34. Yamato Promenade Komingu Kottō Ichi
やまとプロムナード古民具骨董市

LOCATION: Kanagawa-ken, Yamato-shi, area in front of Yamato Station (大和駅前)
NEAREST STATION: Yamato (大和) (1 min.), Odakyū Enoshima/Sōtetsu lines
WHEN: 3rd Saturday, 6:00 A.M.–4:00 P.M.
RAINY WEATHER: Okay
VENDORS: 160   **ESTABLISHED:** 1998
GETTING THERE: The flea market takes place in the immediate vicinity of the station. Take either exit, then look around until you find it.
ADDRESS: Tōzai Promenade, Yamato Eki-mae, Yamato-shi, Kanagawa
神奈川県大和市大和駅前東西プロムナード
CONTACT: 046–267–0077, 090–3579–3828

35. **Sagami Nomi no Ichi**   相模 蚤の市

LOCATION: Kanagawa-ken, Atsugi, Atsugi Shrine (厚木神社)
NEAREST STATION: Hon-Atsugi (本厚木) (6 min.), Odakyū Line
WHEN: 1st Saturday, 5:00 A.M.–4:00 P.M.
RAINY WEATHER: Canceled   **VENDORS:** 40   **ESTABLISHED:** 1974
GETTING THERE: Come out the East Exit, walk about 500 meters along the railway to the T-junction. Turn left and the market will be 200 meters ahead on the right, near the Sagami Ōhashi bridge.
ADDRESS: Atsugi Shrine, 3–8 Atsugi-machi, Atsugi-shi, Kanagawa
神奈川県厚木市厚木町3–8 厚木神社
CONTACT: 046–228–4711, 0462–21–5875 (Atsugi Shrine)

Chiba

36. **Chiba-dera Kottō Ichi**   千葉寺 骨董市

LOCATION: Chiba-ken, Chiba-shi, Chiba-dera Temple (千葉寺)
NEAREST STATION: Chiba-dera (千葉寺) (7 min.), Keisei Chihara Line
WHEN: 3rd Sunday, 8:00 A.M.–4:00 P.M.
RAINY WEATHER: Light rain, okay   **VENDORS:** 40   **ESTABLISHED:** 1990
GETTING THERE: Follow the main street for about 400 meters, until you reach a major intersection. Turn left. The entrance to the grounds of the temple is about 200 meters ahead on the right. Follow the posted banners or flags.
ADDRESS: Chiba-dera, 161 Chiba-dera-machi, Chuo-ku, Chiba-shi
千葉市中央区千葉寺町161 千葉寺
CONTACT: 0476–28–6123, 043–261–3723 (Chiba-dera Temple)

37. **Kottō Antique Fair in Makuhari Messe**
骨董アンティックフェア in 幕張メッセ

LOCATION: Chiba-ken, Makuhari, Makuhari Messe (幕張メッセ)
NEAREST STATION: Kaihin Makuhari (海浜幕張) (5 min.), JR Keiyo Line
WHEN: July (3 days), 10:00 A.M.–5:00 P.M. (first day, noon–5:00 P.M.)
RAINY WEATHER: Held indoors   **VENDORS:** 120   **ESTABLISHED:** 2000
ENTRANCE FEE: ¥1,000 (¥800 in advance)
GETTING THERE: Take the South Exit. Follow the signs from the station to the exhibition center. There are several exhibition halls, but the one where the flea market is held should be clearly marked.
ADDRESS: Makuhari Messe, 2–1, Nakase Mihama-ku, Chiba-shi
千葉市美浜区中瀬 2–1 幕張メッセ
CONTACT: 0276–38–3417, 090–3348–7760, 043–296–0001 (Makuhari Messe)

38. **Makuhari Kottō Ichi**　幕張 骨董市

LOCATION: Chiba-ken, Makuhari, Kaihin Makuhari Station North Exit (海浜幕張駅北口)

NEAREST STATION: Kaihin Makuhari (海浜幕張) (1 min.), JR Keiyo Line

WHEN: 4th Sunday, 7:00 A.M.–4:00 P.M.

RAINY WEATHER: Light rain, okay　VENDORS: 40　ESTABLISHED: 2000

GETTING THERE: The flea market is held in a large open area in front of the North Exit. Go out the North Exit, and you can't miss it.

ADDRESS: Kaihin Makuhari Station, North Exit, Mihama-ku, Chiba-shi
　　　　千葉市美浜区海浜幕張駅北口

CONTACT: 0276–38–3417

39. **Tōgane Kottō Matsuri**　東金骨董祭

LOCATION: Chiba-ken, Tōgane-shi, Jōkōji Temple (上行寺)

NEAREST STATION: Tōgane (東金) (8 min.), JR Tōgane Line

WHEN: 1st Sunday, 6:00 A.M.–3:00 P.M.

RAINY WEATHER: Light rain, okay　VENDORS: 50　ESTABLISHED: 1993

GETTING THERE: Take the West Exit, walk northwest for 100 meters to Route 119. Turn right and continue for about 500 meters to the northeast Katagai Kendō intersection. Walk another 200 meters, then turn left on the street before the court building (簡易裁判所 *kan'i saibansho*). The temple is behind the court.

ADDRESS: Jōkōji Temple, 2366 Tama, Tōgane-shi, Chiba
　　　　千葉県東金市田間2366　上行寺

CONTACT: 0475–53–0199, 0475–52–3208 (Jōkōji Temple)

Saitama

40. **Urawa Juku Furusato Ichi**
浦和宿 ふるさと市

LOCATION: Saitama-ken, Urawa-shi, Tsukinomiya Shrine (調神社)

NEAREST STATION: Urawa (浦和) (7 min.), JR Takasaki/Tōhoku Honsen/Keihin Tōhoku lines

WHEN: 4th Saturday, 7:00 A.M.–4:00 P.M.

RAINY WEATHER: Light rain, okay　VENDORS: 180　ESTABLISHED: 1986

GETTING THERE: Take the West Exit, walk west for 300 meters, and turn left at the major intersection. The shrine will be 700 meters ahead on the left.

ADDRESS: Tsukinomiya Shrine, 3–17–25 Kishi-machi, Urawa-shi, Saitama
　　　　埼玉県浦和市岸町3–17–25　調神社

CONTACT: 048–875–5156, 048–822–2254 (Tsukinomiya Shrine)

41. **Kawagoe Narita Fudō Nomi no Ichi**   川越成田不動 蚤の市

LOCATION: Saitama-ken, Kawagoe-shi, Narita Fudō Temple (成田不動)
NEAREST STATION: Hon-Kawagoe (本川越) (10 min.), Seibu Shinjuku Line •
Additional station: Kawagoe (川越) (12 min.), JR Kawagoe/Tōbu Tōjō lines
WHEN: 28th of month, sunrise–sunset
RAINY WEATHER: Light rain, okay   **VENDORS:** 100   **ESTABLISHED:** 1981
GETTING THERE: From Hon-Kawagoe Station: Take the East Exit, then heading to
the left, go about 500 meters along the street leading to the historic district. Turn
right when you get to the major intersection with a sign pointing to the temple.
Walk about 600 meters. The temple is on the right.
ADDRESS: Narita Fudō Temple, 9–2 Kubo-machi, Kawagoe-shi, Saitama
　　　　　　埼玉県川越市久保町9–2　成田不動
CONTACT: 03–5996–4105, 049–222–0173 (Narita Fudō Temple)

42. **Koedo Kawagoe Charity Kottō Ichi**
小江戸川越 チャリティー骨董市

LOCATION: Saitama-ken, Kawagoe-shi, area in front of Hon-Kawagoe Station
(本川越駅前)
NEAREST STATION: Hon-Kawagoe (本川越) (1 min.), Seibu Shinjuku Line •
Additional station: Kawagoe (川越) (5 min.), JR Kawagoe/Tōbu Tōjō lines
WHEN: 28th of month, sunrise–sunset
RAINY WEATHER: Canceled   **VENDORS:** 50   **ESTABLISHED:** 2001
GETTING THERE: From Hon-Kawagoe Station: Take the East Exit, look to the left,
and you will see the flea market, which takes place in a plaza almost immediately
in front of the station.
ADDRESS: Hon-Kawagoe Station, 2-chōme, Shintomi-chō, Kawagoe-shi, Saitama
　　　　　　埼玉県川越市新富町2丁目　本川越駅前
CONTACT: 049–289–5453

43. **Okegawa-shi Furusato Nomi no Ichi**
桶川市 ふるさと蚤の市

LOCATION: Saitama-ken, Okegawa-shi, Benibana Furusatokan (べに花ふるさ
と館)
NEAREST STATION: Okegawa (桶川), JR Takasaki Line
WHEN: 2nd Sunday, 9:00 A.M.–4:00 P.M.
RAINY WEATHER: Held indoors   **VENDORS:** 30   **ESTABLISHED:** 1999
GETTING THERE: From Okegawa Station take either the Tōbu bus (10 minutes)
for Hosoya Shōbu Shako (細谷菖蒲車庫) and get off at stop called Tenjin Iriguchi
(天神入口), or take the Loopline (east) bus to the Benibana Furusatokan-mae bus
stop, a 15- to 20-minute ride.

ADDRESS: Benibana Furusatokan, 419–1 Kano, Okegawa-shi, Saitama

埼玉県桶川市加納419–1　べに花ふるさと館

CONTACT: 048–729–1611 (Benibana Furusatokan)

44. Sai no Kuni Wayō Kottō Fair in Tokorozawa

彩の国 和洋骨董フェア in 所沢

LOCATION: Saitama-ken, Tokorozawa-shi, Kusunoki Hall (くすのきホール)

NEAREST STATION: Tokorozawa (所沢) (1 min.), Seibu Ikebukuro/Seibu Shinjuku lines

WHEN: Spring (3 days), fall (3 days), 10:00 A.M.–6:00 P.M. (last day 10:00 A.M.–5:00 P.M.)

RAINY WEATHER: Held indoors   VENDORS: 100   ESTABLISHED: 2000

ENTRANCE FEE: ¥500

GETTING THERE: Take the East Exit. Just past the taxi stand, turn right onto the shopping street running perpendicular to the train tracks. Go about 100 meters. Kusonoki Hall is on the right, on the near side of the first traffic light.

ADDRESS: Kusunoki Hall, 1–11–2 Kusunoki-dai, Tokorozawa-shi, Saitama

埼玉県所沢市くすのき台1–11–2　くすのきホール

CONTACT: 03–5996–4105, 042–925–9447 (Kusunoki Hall)

45. Hannō Fukurō Ichi　飯能 梟市

LOCATION: Saitama-ken, Hannō-shi, Hannō Shimin Kaikan (飯能市民会館)

NEAREST STATION: Hannō (飯能), Seibu Ikebukuro Line

WHEN: 1st Sunday, sunrise–sunset

RAINY WEATHER: Light rain, okay   VENDORS: 25   ESTABLISHED: 1994

GETTING THERE: From Hannō Station about 7 minutes by car/taxi. From the North Exit, take a bus heading for the Hannō Shimin Kaikan (飯能市民会館). Get off at the Tenranzan-shita (天覧山下) bus stop.

ADDRESS: Hannō Shimin Kaikan, 226–2 Hannō, Hannō-shi, Saitama

埼玉県飯能市飯能226–2　飯能市民会館

CONTACT: 0429–86–0556, 0429–72–3000 (Hannō Shimin Kaikan)

Tochigi

46. Futaara Kottō Ichi　ふたあら骨董市

LOCATION: Tochigi-ken, Utsunomiya-shi, Futaara-san Shrine (二荒山神社)

NEAREST STATION: Utsunomiya (宇都宮) (10 min.), JR Utsunomiya/Tōhoku Shinkansen lines • *Additional station:* Tōbu Utsunomiya (東武宇都宮) (7 min.), Tōbu Utsunomiya Line

WHEN: 4th Saturday, 8:00 A.M.–sunset (not held in October)

RAINY WEATHER: Light rain, okay   **VENDORS:** 20–30   **ESTABLISHED:** 2000

GETTING THERE: From Utsunomiya Station: Follow the main road heading from the station west for about a kilometer, crossing a river, passing a hospital, and passing through an intersection. The shrine is on the right.

ADDRESS: Futaara-san Shrine, 1–1–1 Baba Dōri, Utsunomiya-shi, Tochigi
　　　　　栃木県宇都宮市馬場通り1–1–1　二荒山神社

CONTACT: 03–5996–4105, 028–622–5271 (Futaara-san Shrine)

47. Ōsaki Jinja O-takara Kottō Ichi　大前神社 お宝骨董市

LOCATION: Tochigi-ken, Mooka-shi, Ōsaki Shrine (大前神社)

NEAREST STATION: Kita-Mooka (北真岡), Mooka Line

WHEN: 2nd Sunday (in November, changes to 4th Sunday), 8:00 A.M.–sunset

RAINY WEATHER: Light rain, okay   **VENDORS:** 150   **ESTABLISHED:** 1996

GETTING THERE: From Kita-Mooka or Mooka: Take the free shuttle bus. From Kita-Mooka Station: Walk west along the tracks, turn right after seeing the blue railway bridge. The shrine is in the direction of the forest (don't cross the intersection) along the Gogyō River and Route 294.

ADDRESS: Ōsaki Shrine, 937 Tōgō, Mooka-shi, Tochigi
　　　　　栃木県真岡市東郷937　大前神社

CONTACT: 0285–84–8600, 0285–82–2509 (Ōsaki Shrine)

Ibaraki

48. Ichinoya Yasaka Jinja Kottō Nomi no Ichi
一の矢八坂神社 骨董蚤の市

LOCATION: Ibaraki-ken, Tsukuba-shi, Ichinoya Yasaka Shrine (一の矢八坂神社)

NEAREST STATION: Tokyo Station → bus (1 hour)

WHEN: 4th Sunday, 8:00 A.M.–4:00 P.M.

RAINY WEATHER: Okay   **VENDORS:** 140   **ESTABLISHED:** 1997

GETTING THERE: From Yaesu Minami (South Exit) exit of Tokyo Station, take the JR bus to Tsukubagō (つくば号). Get off at stop called Tsukuba Center (つくばセンター). Takes 1 hour (one-way fare, ¥1,250).

ADDRESS: Ichinoya Yasaka Shrine, 2617 Tamatori, Tsukuba-shi, Ibaraki
　　　　　茨城県つくば市玉取2617　一の矢八坂神社

CONTACT: 0298–42–7689, 0298–64–1132 (Ichinoya Yasaka Shrine)

49. Kuri no Ie Nomi no Ichi　栗の家 蚤の市

LOCATION: Ibaraki-ken, Iwama, Kuri no Ie Garden (栗の家庭園)

NEAREST STATION: Iwama (岩間), JR Jōban Line
WHEN: 3rd Sunday, 6:00 A.M.–4:30 P.M.
RAINY WEATHER: Light rain, okay   VENDORS: 65   ESTABLISHED: 1996
GETTING THERE: From Iwama Station about 8 minutes by car/taxi.
ADDRESS: Kuri no Ie Garden, 1285 Haji, Iwama-chō, Nishi-Ibaraki-gun, Ibaraki
　　　　　茨城県西茨城郡岩間町土師1285　栗の家
CONTACT: 03–3311–1609, 0299–45–5124 (Kuri no Ie)

Gunma

50. Takasaki Zenkoku Kottō Nomi no Ichi
高崎 全国骨董蚤の市

LOCATION: Gunma-ken, Takasaki-shi, Tonya-machi Center (問屋町センター)
NEAREST STATION: Takasaki (高崎), JR Takasaki/Hachikō lines
WHEN: April (3 days), December (3 days), 10:00 A.M.–6:00 P.M. (last day 10:00 A.M.–4:00 P.M.)
RAINY WEATHER: Held indoors   VENDORS: 80   ESTABLISHED: 1983
GETTING THERE: From Takasaki Station about 12 minutes by car/taxi (about ¥1,200). Bus service is infrequent.
ADDRESS: Tonya-machi Center, 2–7 Tonya-machi, Takasaki-shi, Gunma
　　　　　群馬県高崎市問屋町2–7　問屋町センター
CONTACT: 027–324–0703, 027–361–8243 (Tonya-machi Center)

51. Takasaki Tamachi Kottō Kaidō　高崎田町 骨董街道

LOCATION: Gunma-ken, Takasaki-shi, Tamachi Ōdōri (田町大通り)
NEAREST STATION: Takasaki (高崎) (10 min.), JR Takasaki Line
WHEN: Last Sunday, sunrise–sunset
RAINY WEATHER: Light rain, okay   VENDORS: 65   ESTABLISHED: 1984
GETTING THERE: Come out the West Exit (the side with the roundabout) and go straight west down the large avenue. Turn right at the first signal (about 400 meters down). The flea market begins about 500 meters down, around Tamachi intersection.
ADDRESS: Tamachi Ōdōri, Tamachi, Takasaki-shi, Gunma
　　　　　群馬県高崎市田町田町大通り
CONTACT: 027–324–5040

52. Maebashi Zenkoku Kottō Nomi no Ichi
前橋 全国骨董蚤の市

LOCATION: Gunma-ken, Maebashi-shi, Kensetsu Kaikan (建設会館)
NEAREST STATION: Shin-Maebashi (新前橋), JR Jōetsu Line

WHEN: February (3 days), August (3 days), 10:00 A.M.–6:00 P.M.

RAINY WEATHER: Held indoors   **VENDORS:** 30   **ESTABLISHED:** 1990

GETTING THERE: From Shin-Maebashi Station about 6 minutes by car/taxi. Bus service is infrequent.

ADDRESS: Kensetsu Kaikan, 2–5–3 Moto Sōja-machi, Maebashi-shi, Gunma

群馬県前橋市元総社町2–5–3　建設会館

CONTACT: 027–324–0703, 027–252–1666 (Kensetsu Kaikan)

53. Kiryū Tenmangū Komingu Kottō Ichi
桐生天満宮 古民具骨董市

LOCATION: Gunma-ken, Kiryū-shi, Kiryū Tenmangū Shrine (桐生天満宮)

NEAREST STATION: Kiryū (桐生), JR Ryōmō Line

WHEN: 1st Saturday, sunrise–5:00 P.M.

RAINY WEATHER: Light rain, okay   **VENDORS:** 100   **ESTABLISHED:** 1993

GETTING THERE: From Kiryū Station about 9 minutes by car/taxi. On foot, walk north for 1.5 kilometers to the shrine. Or from the North Exit board a bus bound for Umeda (梅田) or Kiryū Joshiko-mae (桐生女子高前) and get off at Gundai Seimon-mae (郡大正門前) bus stop. The shrine is in front of the bus stop.

ADDRESS: Kiryū Tenmangū Shrine, 1–2–1 Tenjin-machi, Kiryū-shi, Gunma

群馬県桐生市天神町1–2–1　桐生天満宮

CONTACT: 0270–23–6582 (Kiryū Tenmangū Shrine)

54. Obiki Inari Kottō Ichi   尾曳稲荷 骨董市

LOCATION: Gunma-ken, Tatebayashi-shi, Obiki Inari Shrine (尾曳稲荷神社)

NEAREST STATION: Tatebayashi (館林) (20 min.), Tōbu Isezaki Line

WHEN: 3rd Saturday, 5:00 A.M.–4:00 P.M.

RAINY WEATHER: Light rain, okay   **VENDORS:** 50–60   **ESTABLISHED:** 1999

GETTING THERE: Walk west for about 1.2 kilometers, passing the city office. The shrine is in Obiki Park.

ADDRESS: Obiki Inari Shrine, 10–1 Obiki-chō, Tatebayashi-shi, Gunma

群馬県館林市尾曳町10–1　尾曳稲荷神社

CONTACT: 0276–72–4856, 0276–72–1293 (Obiki Inari Shrine)

KYOTO/OSAKA AND THE KANSAI AREA

Kyoto

55. **Tōji Garakuta Ichi**　東寺 ガラクタ市

LOCATION: Kyoto, Tōji Temple (東寺)
NEAREST STATION: Tōji (東寺) (5 min.), Kintetsu Kyoto Line
WHEN: 1st Sunday, 5:00 A.M.–4:00 P.M.
RAINY WEATHER: Okay　**VENDORS:** 80　**ESTABLISHED:** 1982
GETTING THERE: Follow the main street (Route 1) west for about 350 meters. The entrance to the grounds of the temple is on the right.
ADDRESS: Tōji Temple, 1 Kujō-machi, Minami-ku, Kyoto
　　　　　　京都市南区九条町1　東寺
CONTACT: 0771–22–3992, 075–691–3325 (Tōji Temple)

56. **Tōji Kōbō Ichi**　東寺 弘法市

LOCATION: Kyoto, Tōji Temple (東寺)
NEAREST STATION: Tōji (東寺) (5 min.), Kintetsu Kyoto Line
WHEN: 21st of month, 5:00 A.M.–4:00 P.M.
RAINY WEATHER: Okay
VENDORS: 1,250 (most of the vendors sell food or everyday merchandise, not antiques)
GETTING THERE: Follow the main street (Route 1) west for about 350 meters. The entrance to the grounds of the temple is on the right.

ADDRESS: Tōji Temple, 1 Kujō-machi, Minami-ku, Kyoto
京都市南区九条町1　東寺
CONTACT: 0771–22–3992

57. **Tōji Shōgatsu Ichi**　東寺 正月市

LOCATION: Kyoto, Tōji Temple (東寺)
NEAREST STATION: Tōji (東寺) (5 min.), Kintetsu Kyoto Line
WHEN: January 1–4, 5:00 A.M.–4:00 P.M.
RAINY WEATHER: Okay
VENDORS: 50–60　ESTABLISHED: 1992
GETTING THERE: Follow the main street (Route 1) west for about 350 meters. The entrance to the grounds of the temple is on the right.
ADDRESS: Tōji Temple, 1 Kujō-machi, Minami-ku, Kyoto
京都市南区九条町1　東寺
CONTACT: 0771–22–3992

58. **Kitano Tenmangū Tenjin Ichi**　北野天満宮 天神市

LOCATION: Kyoto, Kitano Tenmangū Shrine (北野天満宮)
NEAREST STATION: Kyoto (京都), JR Tōkaidō Line • *Additional station:* Ōmiya (大宮), Hankyū Kyoto Line
WHEN: 25th of month, 6:00 A.M.–4:00 P.M.
RAINY WEATHER: Okay　VENDORS: 200
GETTING THERE: From Kyoto Station: Take bus no. 55 to Kitano Tenmangū-mae bus stop (takes 30 minutes). From Ōmiya Station take taxi (15 minutes).
ADDRESS: Kitano Tenmangū Shrine, Kitano Bakuro-chō, Kamigyō-ku, Kyoto
京都市上京区北野馬喰町　北野天満宮
CONTACT: 075–811–3685, 075–461–0005 (Kitano Tenmangū Shrine)

59. **Kyoto Dai Kottō Matsuri**　京都大骨董祭

LOCATION: Kyoto, Pulse Plaza (パルスプラザ)
NEAREST STATION: Takeda (竹田), Karasuma subway line
WHEN: March (3 days), June (3 days), November (3 days), 10:00 A.M.–6:00 P.M. (last day 10:00 A.M.–5:00 P.M.)
RAINY WEATHER: Held indoors
VENDORS: 250　ESTABLISHED: 1994
GETTING THERE: Take the free shuttle bus from West Exit of Takeda Station.
ADDRESS: Pulse Plaza, 5 Takeda-Tobadono-machi, Fushimi-ku, Kyoto
京都市伏見区竹田鳥羽殿町5　パルスプラザ
CONTACT: 077–522–2307 (吾目堂), 075–611–0011 (Pulse Plaza)

60. **Zenkoku Kottōya Daishūgō in Kyoto**
全国骨董屋大集合 in 京都

LOCATION: Kyoto, Pulse Plaza (パルスプラザ)
NEAREST STATION: Takeda (竹田), Karasuma subway line
WHEN: Winter (3 days), summer (3 days), 10:00 A.M.–5:00 P.M. (last day, 10:00 A.M.–4:00 P.M.)
RAINY WEATHER: Held indoors   VENDORS: 250   ESTABLISHED: 1994
GETTING THERE: Take the free shuttle bus from the West Exit of Takeda Station.
ADDRESS: Pulse Plaza, 5 Takeda-Tobadono-machi, Fushimi-ku, Kyoto
　　　　　京都市伏見区竹田鳥羽殿町5　パルスプラザ
CONTACT: 0771–26–3603, 075–611–0011 (Pulse Plaza)

Osaka

61. **O-hatsu Tenjin Nomi no Ichi**　お初天神 蚤の市

LOCATION: Osaka, Tsuyu Tenjin Shrine (露天神)
NEAREST STATION: Osaka (大阪) (5 min.), JR Tōkaidō Line • *Additional station:* Umeda (梅田) (5 min.), Hankyū/Hanshin/Midōsuji subway lines
WHEN: 1st Friday, 3rd Friday, sunrise–sunset
RAINY WEATHER: Okay   VENDORS: 35   ESTABLISHED: 1980
GETTING THERE: Exit Osaka Station through the Southeast Exit to Midōsuji Street, a wide avenue running by the east side of the station. Turn right (south) and walk for about 250 meters. Turn left on the narrow street with the Adachi Jewelry store on the corner. Tsuyu Tenjin Shrine is at the end of the street.
ADDRESS: Tsuyu Tenjin Shrine, 2–5–4 Sonezaki, Kita-ku, Osaka
　　　　　大阪市北区曽根崎2-5-4　露天神
CONTACT: 06–6790–3781, 06–6311–0895 (Tsuyu Tenjin Shrine)

62. **Ikutama Nomi no Ichi**　いくたま 蚤の市

LOCATION: Osaka, Ikutama Shrine (生国魂神社)
NEAREST STATION: Tanimachi 9-chōme (谷町九丁目) (4 min.), Tanimachi subway line
WHEN: 8th of month, 8:00 A.M.–4:00 P.M.
RAINY WEATHER: Okay   VENDORS: 25   ESTABLISHED: 1990
GETTING THERE: Follow the main street (Sennichi-mae Dōri 千日前通) to the west for about 200 meters. Take the second left. Go about 150 meters, passing through an intersection. The entrance to the grounds of the shrine is on the right.
ADDRESS: Ikutama Shrine, 13–9 Ikutama-chō, Tennōji-ku, Osaka
　　　　　大阪市天王寺区生玉町13-9　生国魂神社
CONTACT: 072–823–2256, 06–6771–0002 (Ikutama Shrine)

63. **Shitennōji Daishi-e**   四天王寺 大師会

LOCATION: Osaka, Shitennōji Temple (四天王寺)
NEAREST STATION: Shitennōji-mae Yūhigaoka (四天王寺前夕陽ヶ丘) (5 min.), Tanimachi subway line
WHEN: 21st of month, 9:00 A.M.–sunset
RAINY WEATHER: Okay   **VENDORS:** 400
GETTING THERE: Follow the main street (Tanimachi-suji) to the south, for about 500 meters. Turn left at Tennōji-Nishimon-mae crossing. The market is 300 meters down the road on the left.
ADDRESS: Shitennōji Temple, 1–11–18 Shitennōji, Tennōji-ku, Osaka
　　　　　　大阪市天王寺区四天王寺1–11–18　四天王寺
CONTACT: 06–6771–0066 (Shitennōji Temple)

64. **Osaka Kottō Matsuri**   大阪骨董祭

LOCATION: Osaka, My Dome Osaka (マイドーム大阪)
NEAREST STATION: Tanimachi 4-chōme (谷町四丁目) (7 min.), Tanimachi subway line • *Additional station:* Sakaisuji Honmachi (堺筋本町) (7 min.), Sakaisuji/Chūō subway lines
WHEN: April (3 days), July (3 days), October (3 days), 10:00 A.M.–5:00 P.M. (last day 10:00 A.M.–4:00 P.M.)
RAINY WEATHER: Held indoors   **VENDORS:** 120   **ESTABLISHED:** 1990
GETTING THERE: From Tanimachi 4-chōme Station: Take the exit signposted My Dome Osaka. Follow the major street (Tanimachi-suji) north. Turn left at the Tanimachi 3-chōme intersection on to Honmachi Dōri. Go 400 meters, then turn right at Uchi Honmachi 2-chōme crossing. The dome is about 100 meters ahead on the left.
ADDRESS: My Dome Osaka, 2–5 Honmachi-bashi, Chūō-ku, Osaka
　　　　　　大阪市中央区本町橋2–5　マイドーム大阪
CONTACT: 072–823–2256, 06–6947–4324 (My Dome Osaka)

65. **Sekai Kottō Fair in Osaka Dome**
世界骨董フェア in 大阪ドーム

LOCATION: Osaka, Osaka Dome (大阪ドーム)
NEAREST STATION: Osaka Dome-mae Chiyozaki (大阪ドーム前千代崎) (3 min.), Nagahori Tsurumi Ryokuchi subway line • *Additional stations:* Taishō (大正) (7 min.), JR Osaka Kanjō Line • Kujō (九条) (9 min.), Chūō subway line
WHEN: February (2 days), 10:00 A.M.–5:00 P.M.
RAINY WEATHER: Held indoors   **VENDORS:** 300   **ESTABLISHED:** 1999
GETTING THERE: From Osaka Dome-mae Chiyozaki Station: Take the exit signposted Osaka Dome. The dome is clearly visible from the station, at a distance of about 250 meters as the crow flies.

ADDRESS: Osaka Dome, Naka 2–1, 3-chōme Chiyozaki, Nishi-ku, Osaka

大阪市西区千代崎3丁目中2–1　大阪ドーム

CONTACT: 072–823–2256, 06　6586　0106 (Osaka Dome)

66. Dōmyōji Tenmangū Nomi no Ichi　道明寺天満宮 蚤の市

LOCATION: Osaka, Dōmyōji Tenmangū Shrine (道明寺天満宮)

NEAREST STATION: Dōmyōji (道明寺) (5 min.), Kintetsu Minami Osaka Line

WHEN: 25th of month, 6:00 A.M.–4:00 P.M.

RAINY WEATHER: Okay　**VENDORS:** 15　**ESTABLISHED:** 1997

GETTING THERE: On the west side of the station.

ADDRESS: Dōmyōji Tenmangū, 1 Dōmyōji, Fujii-dera-shi, Osaka

大阪府藤井寺市道明寺1　道明寺天満宮

CONTACT: 06–6927–8933, 090–3872–2373, 0729–53–2525 (Dōmyōji Shrine)

67. Sakai Dai Kottō Matsuri　堺 大骨董祭

LOCATION: Osaka, Minami Osaka Jiba Sangyō Shinkō Center (南大阪地場産業振興センター)

NEAREST STATION: Nakamozu (中百舌鳥) (5 min.), Midōsuji subway line/Nankai Kōya Line

WHEN: Spring (2 days), fall (2 days), 10:00 A.M.–5:00 P.M.

RAINY WEATHER: Held indoors　**VENDORS:** 85　**ESTABLISHED:** 1988

GETTING THERE: From the subway station: Walk east for about 50 meters, then turn left. The Center will be 200 meters down on the right.

ADDRESS: Minami Osaka Jiba Sangyō Shinkō Center, 183 Nagasone-machi, Naka-mozu, Sakai-shi, Osaka

大阪府堺市中百舌鳥長曽根町183 南大阪地場産業振興センター

CONTACT: 072–261–6000 (Sakai Bijutsushō Kumiai), 072–255–0111

Kobe

68. Bazaar in Rokkō　バザール in 六甲

LOCATION: Kobe, Gokoku Shrine (護国神社)

NEAREST STATION: Rokkō (六甲), Hankyū Kobe Line

WHEN: 4th Sunday, 8:00 A.M.–4:00 P.M.

RAINY WEATHER: Light rain, okay　**VENDORS:** 50–60　**ESTABLISHED:** 1984

GETTING THERE: From Rokkō Station take the Kobe City bus bound for San-nomiya (三宮). Get off at the stop called Gokoku Jinja-mae (護国神社前).

ADDRESS: Gokoku Shrine, 4–5–1 Shinohara Kita-machi, Nada-ku, Kobe-shi

神戸市灘区篠原北町4–5–1　護国神社

CONTACT: 078–871–4484, 078–882–1700 (Gokoku Shrine)

69. **Kobe Dai Kottō Matsuri**　神戸大骨董祭

LOCATION: Kobe, Kobe Fashion Mart (神戸ファッションマート)
NEAREST STATION: Island Center (アイランドセンター) (1 min.), Rokkō Liner (accessible via Sumiyoshi Station on JR Kobe Line)
WHEN: Spring (3 days), fall (3 days), 10:00 A.M.–6:00 P.M. (last day 10:00 A.M.–5:00 P.M.)
RAINY WEATHER: Held indoors　**VENDORS:** 150　**ESTABLISHED:** 1994
GETTING THERE: Follow the signs to Kobe Fashion Mart, an exhibition center located adjacent to the station.
ADDRESS: Kobe Fashion Mart, 6–9 Kōyō-chō Naka, Higashi-Nada-ku, Kobe-shi
　　　　神戸市東灘区向洋町中6–9　神戸ファッションマート
CONTACT: 077–522–2307, 078–857–8001 (Kobe Fashion Mart)

70. **Suma-dera Nomi no Ichi**　須磨寺 蚤の市

LOCATION: Kobe, Suma-dera Temple (須磨寺)
NEAREST STATION: Suma (須磨), JR Kobe Line • *Additional station:* Suma-dera (須磨寺), Sanyō Dentetsu Line
WHEN: 1st Sunday (except January), 7:00 A.M.–4:00 P.M.
RAINY WEATHER: rescheduled for 2nd Sunday
VENDORS: 50　**ESTABLISHED:** 1981
GETTING THERE: From Suma-dera Station: Take the exit signposted Suma-dera. Follow the street that runs perpendicular to the train tracks north for about 500 meters, until you reach a T-junction. Turn left at the T-junction. Walk about 150 meters, until the road ends. The entrance to the grounds of the temple is on the right. From Suma Station about 7 minutes by car/taxi.
ADDRESS: Suma-dera Temple, 4–6–8 Suma-dera-machi, Suma-ku, Kobe-shi
　　　　神戸市須磨区須磨寺町4–6–8　須磨寺
CONTACT: 078–361–1361, 078–731–0416 (Suma-dera Temple)

Nara

71. **Kōriyama Nomi no Ichi**　郡山 蚤の市

LOCATION: Nara, Sotobori Park (外堀公園)
NEAREST STATION: Kōriyama (郡山) (5 min.), JR Kansai Line
WHEN: 2nd Sunday, 7:00 A.M.–4:00 P.M.
RAINY WEATHER: Okay　**VENDORS:** 30　**ESTABLISHED:** 1998
GETTING THERE: About 200 meters from the west side of the station.
ADDRESS: Sotobori Kōen (Park), Takada-chō, Yamato Kōriyama-shi, Nara
　　　　奈良県大和郡山市高田町　外堀公園 （外堀緑地）
CONTACT: 0744–22–0803

72. **Miwa Jinja Tōzai Kobutsu Kottō Ichi**
三輪神社 東西古物骨董市

LOCATION: Nara, Miwa Shrine (三輪神社)

NEAREST STATION: Miwa (三輪) (3 min.), JR Sakurai Line

WHEN: 2nd Sunday, 5:00 A.M.–4:00 P.M.

RAINY WEATHER: Light rain, okay   **VENDORS:** 25   **ESTABLISHED:** 1997

GETTING THERE: Come out the exit and turn right 100 meters down the road. Cross the tracks and the shrine will be 100 meters down on the right.

ADDRESS: Miwa Shrine, Miwa-machi, Sakurai-shi, Nara
    奈良県桜井市三輪町　三輪神社

CONTACT: 06–6781–0426, 0744–42–6633 (Miwa Shrine)

73. **Shigisan Tora no Ichi**   信貴山 寅の市

LOCATION: Nara, Chōgo Sonshiji Temple (朝護孫子寺)

NEAREST STATION: Shigisan-shita (信貴山下), Kintetsu Ikoma Line

WHEN: 3rd Sunday, 9:00 A.M.–4:00 P.M.

RAINY WEATHER: Canceled   **VENDORS:** 40   **ESTABLISHED:** 2000

GETTING THERE: Take the bus bound for Shigisan (信貴山) to the end of line.

ADDRESS: Chōgo Sonshiji Temple, 2280–1 Shigisan, Heguri-chō, Ikoma-gun, Nara
    奈良県生駒郡平群町信貴山2280–1　朝後孫子寺

CONTACT: 0745–72–2277 (Chōgo Sonshiji Temple)

Shiga

74. **Koedo Hikone no Kottō Ichi**
小江戸彦根の骨董市

LOCATION: Shiga-ken, Hikone-shi, Hikone Castle Ninomaru (彦根二ノ丸)

NEAREST STATION: Hikone (彦根) (15 min.), JR Tōkaidō Line

WHEN: 3rd Saturday, 3rd Sunday, 10:00 A.M.–5:00 P.M.

RAINY WEATHER: Okay   **VENDORS:** 25   **ESTABLISHED:** 1994

GETTING THERE: Take the exit signposted Hikone Castle. Follow the main street running perpendicular to the train tracks, heading northwest for about 500 meters, until you reach a T-junction. Turn left at the T-junction, go about 100 meters, then turn right. The entrance to the grounds of the castle is about 250 meters straight ahead.

ADDRESS: Hikone Castle, 1–1 Konki-chō, Hikone-shi, Shiga
    滋賀県彦根市金亀町1–1　彦根城

CONTACT: 0749–23–0001 (Hikone Kankō Kyōkai), 0749–22–2742 (Hikone Castle)

OTHER REGIONS

NORTHERN AREA

Hokkaidō

75. Gokoku Jinja Kita no Nomi no Ichi
護国神社 北の蚤の市

LOCATION: Hokkaidō, Sapporo-shi, Gokoku Shrine (護国神社)
NEAREST STATION: Horohirabashi (幌平橋) (1 min.), Nanboku subway line
WHEN: 1st Sunday (December through March), 9:00 A.M.–4:00 P.M.
RAINY WEATHER: Okay; snow okay   VENDORS: 15   ESTABLISHED: 1999
GETTING THERE: Take the exit signposted Gokoku Shrine. Follow the street that runs perpendicular to the train tracks south, then west, for about 150 meters. The entrance to the grounds of the shrine is on the right, past the river and just after some tennis courts.
ADDRESS: Gokoku Shrine, 1 Nishi 5-chōme, Minami 15-jō, Chūō-ku, Sapporo-shi
札幌市中央区南15条西5丁目1　護国神社
CONTACT: 011–814–6070, 011–511–5421 (Gokoku Shrine)

76. Toyohira Jinja Kottō Aozora Ichi
豊平神社 骨董青空市

LOCATION: Hokkaidō, Sapporo-shi, Toyohira Shrine (豊平神社)
NEAREST STATION: Toyohira Kōen (豊平公園) (7 min.), Toho subway line

WHEN: Last Sunday, April to November (may change), 9:00 A.M.–4:30 P.M.

RAINY WEATHER: Light rain, okay

VENDORS: 25   **ESTABLISHED:** 1997

GETTING THERE: Take the exit signposted Toyohira Park. Heading north, follow the street that runs along the park for about 250 meters, then make the first left. Go to the end of the park, then go one more block. Turn left. The entrance to the grounds of the shrine is on the right.

ADDRESS: Toyohira Shrine, 1–18, 13-chōme, Toyohira 4-jō, Toyohira-ku, Sapporo-shi
　　　　　札幌市豊平区豊平4条13丁目1–18　豊平神社

CONTACT: 011–812–8200, 011–811–1049 (Toyohira Shrine)

77. Obihiro Komingu Kottō Ichi　帯広 古民具骨董市

LOCATION: Hokkaidō, Obihiro-shi, Obihiro Myōjin Taisha Shrine (帯広明神大社)

NEAREST STATION: Obihiro (帯広), JR Nemuro Line

WHEN: 1st Saturday, 1st Sunday, 9:00 A.M.–4:00 P.M.

RAINY WEATHER: Canceled

VENDORS: 11   **ESTABLISHED:** 1998

GETTING THERE: From Obihiro Station about 8 minutes by car/taxi. Or walk north on Route 241 to Route 38 (1.2 kilometers), then turn left. Make a right at the third street (Nishi 4-jō). Walk 300 meters to the T-junction, and turn left. The shrine is down on the right.

ADDRESS: Obihiro Myōjin Taisha Shrine, 4–14 Nishi 4-jō Kita, Obihiro-shi, Hokkaidō
　　　　　北海道帯広市西4条北4丁目14　帯広明神大社

CONTACT: 0155–33–1171, 0155–24–1329 (Obihiro Myōjin Taisha)

Akita

78. Tōri-machi Shōfuku Inari Kottō Ichi
通町招福稲荷 骨董市

LOCATION: Akita-ken, Akita-shi, Shōfuku Inari Shrine (招福稲荷神社)

NEAREST STATION: Akita (秋田), JR Ōu Line

WHEN: 4th Saturday (April through October), 10:00 A.M.–sunset

RAINY WEATHER: Light rain, okay

VENDORS: 15   **ESTABLISHED:** 1996

GETTING THERE: From Akita Station about 7 minutes by car/taxi. Or walk straight west on Hirokōji Dōri (広小路通り) for about 800 meters, then turn right at Hirokōji-nishi intersection. Turn left at Torimachi-bashi (通町橋) intersection (about 200 meters) and then turn right just before the signal.

ADDRESS: Shōfuku Inari Shrine, 3 Tōri-machi, Hodono, Akita-shi, Akita
　　　　　秋田県秋田市保戸野通町3　招福稲荷神社

CONTACT: 018–832–3910

Yamagata

79. Suwa Jinja Komingu Kottō Ichi   諏訪神社 古民具骨董市

LOCATION: Yamagata-ken, Yamagata-shi, Suwa Shrine (諏訪神社)
NEAREST STATION: Yamagata (山形), JR Ōu Line
WHEN: 1st Sunday, 8:00 A.M.–4:00 P.M.
RAINY WEATHER: Light rain, okay   **VENDORS:** 20   **ESTABLISHED:** 1987
GETTING THERE: From Yamagata Station about 9 minutes by car/taxi. Walk straight east on the main street. The market is on the left about 800 meters down.
ADDRESS: Suwa Shrine, 1–1–55 Suwa-machi, Yamagata-shi, Yamagata
　　　　　山形県山形市諏訪町1–1–55　諏訪神社
CONTACT: 022–363–0927, 023–622–6358 (Suwa Shrine)

80. Yonezawa Machi no Hiroba Komingu Kottō Nomi no Ichi   米沢まちの広場 古民具骨董蚤の市

LOCATION: Yamagata-ken, Yonezawa-shi, Yonezawa Machi no Hiroba (米沢まちの広場)
NEAREST STATION: Yonezawa (米沢), JR Ōu Line
WHEN: 2nd Sunday (April through November), 7:00 A.M.–4:00 P.M.
RAINY WEATHER: Okay   **VENDORS:** 20   **ESTABLISHED:** 1999
GETTING THERE: From Yonezawa Station about 7 minutes by car/taxi. Emerging from the station, there are a number of large streets. Look for a sign directing you toward Hotel Sunroute or ask someone to point out the correct street. Walk west on the street for about 1.5 kilometers past the Suminoe-bashi bridge (住之江橋; about 700 meters). The Machi no Hiroba is in front of the hotel.
ADDRESS: Yonezawa Machi no Hiroba, 1–3025 Chuo, Yonezawa-shi, Yamagata
　　　　　山形県米沢市中央1–3025　米沢まちの広場
CONTACT: 090–2956–8735

Miyagi

81. Sendai Charity Komingu Kottō Ichi
仙台 チャリティー古民具骨董市

LOCATION: Miyagi-ken, Sendai-shi, Sendai Wasse (仙台ワッセ)
NEAREST STATION: Yaotome (八乙女) (7 min.), subway
WHEN: Spring (2 days), fall (2 days), 10:00 A.M.–6:00 P.M.
RAINY WEATHER: Held indoors   **VENDORS:** 50   **ESTABLISHED:** 2001
GETTING THERE: Come out Exit 1-North, walk about 50 meters, turn left, then turn left again at the first major intersection. The Sendai Wasse convention hall is 500 meters down on the left.

82. Sendai Daikannon Komingu Kottō Ichi
仙台大観音 古民具骨董市

LOCATION: Miyagi-ken, Sendai-shi, Sendai Daikannon (仙台大観音)
NEAREST STATION: Yaotome (八乙女), subway
WHEN: 3rd Sunday, 10:00 A.M.–4:00 P.M.
RAINY WEATHER: Held indoors　VENDORS: 15–20　ESTABLISHED: 1992
GETTING THERE: From Yaotome Station take bus for Nakayama (中山). Get off at stop called Jusco-mae (ジャスコ前). The ride takes 10 to 15 minutes.
ADDRESS: Sendai Daikannon, 31–7, Minami Nakayama, Sanezawa, Izumi-ku, Sendai-shi, Miyagi　宮城県仙台市泉区実沢南中山31–7　仙台大観音
CONTACT: 022–363–0927, 022–278–1227 (Sendai Daikannon)

83. Sendai Komingu Kottō Aozora Ichi
仙台 古民具骨董青空市

LOCATION: Miyagi-ken, Sendai-shi, Tōshōgū Shrine (東照宮)
NEAREST STATION: Tōshōgū (東照宮) (2 min.), JR Senzan Line
WHEN: 4th Sunday, 8:00 A.M.–3:00 P.M.
RAINY WEATHER: Light rain, okay　VENDORS: 20　ESTABLISHED: 1984
GETTING THERE: Just north of the station.
ADDRESS: Tōshōgū Shrine, 1–6–1 Tōshōgū, Aoba-ku, Sendai-shi, Miyagi
宮城県仙台市青葉区東照宮1–6–1　東照宮
CONTACT: 0191–23–1888, 022–234–3247 (Tōshōgū Shrine)

84. Sendai Zenkoku Kottō Nomi no Ichi
仙台 全国骨董蚤の市

LOCATION: Miyagi-ken, Sendai-shi, Aztec Museum (アズテックミュージアム)
NEAREST STATION: Minami Sendai (南仙台) (10 min.), JR Tōhoku Line
WHEN: March (3 days), July (3 days), November (3 days), 10:00 A.M.–5:00 P.M.
RAINY WEATHER: Held indoors　VENDORS: 50　ESTABLISHED: 1989
GETTING THERE: Take the East Exit. Walk straight past Route 4, go another 500 meters to the next large intersection (Shiromaru) at the R4 Bypass. The Aztec Museum can be seen from the road.
ADDRESS: Aztec Museum, 18 Suginoshita, Nakata-machi, Taihaku-ku, Sendai-shi, Miyagi　宮城県仙台市太白区中田町杉の下18　アズテックミュージアム
CONTACT: 027–324–0703, 022–241–7111 (Aztec Museum)

85. **Kōriyama Kobijutsu Kottō Ichi**   郡山 古美術骨董市

LOCATION: Fukushima-ken, Kōriyama-shi, Minami Tōhoku Sōgō Oroshi Center (南東北総合卸センター)

NEAREST STATION: Kōriyama (郡山), JR Tōhoku Line

WHEN: Spring (3 days), fall (3 days), 10:00 A.M.–5:00 P.M. (last day 10:00 A.M.–4:00 P.M.)

RAINY WEATHER: Held indoors   VENDORS: 45   ESTABLISHED: 1996

GETTING THERE: From Kōriyama Station take bus for Oroshiuri Danchi (卸売団地). Get off at end of line.

ADDRESS: Minami Tōhoku Sōgō Oroshi Center, 1–1–1 Oroshi, Kikuta-chō, Kōriyama-shi, Fukushima   福島県郡山市喜久田町卸1–1–1 南東北総合卸センター

CONTACT: 024–534–8477, 024–959–6001 (Minami Tōhoku Sōgō Oroshi Center)

CENTRAL AREA

Niigata

86. **Echigo Nagaoka Kottō Ōichi**   越後・長岡骨董大市

LOCATION: Niigata-ken, Nagaoka-shi, Haibu Nagaoka (Nagaoka Sangyō Kōryū Kaikan) (ハイブ長岡［長岡産業交流会館］)

NEAREST STATION: Nagaoka (長岡), JR Jōetsu Line

WHEN: November (3 days), 10:00 A.M.–6:00 P.M. (last day 10:00 A.M.–5:00 P.M.)

RAINY WEATHER: Held indoors   VENDORS: 150   ESTABLISHED: 1992

GETTING THERE: From Nagaoka Station take bus for Kenritsu Kindai Bijutsukan (県立近代美術館). Get off at stop called Nagaoka Sangyō Kōryū Kaikan (長岡産業交流会館).

ADDRESS: Haibu Nagaoka, 315 Terashima-machi, Nagaoka-shi, Niigata
　　　　　新潟県長岡市寺島町315 ハイブ長岡

CONTACT: 03–5996–4105, 0258–27–8812 (Haibu Nagaoka)

87. **Niigata Kottō Ōichi**   新潟骨董大市

LOCATION: Niigata-ken, Niigata-shi, Niigata-chiiki Sangyō Shinkō Center (新潟地域産業振興センター)

NEAREST STATION: Niigata (新潟), JR Jōetsu Line

WHEN: March (3 days), September (3 days), 10:00 A.M.–6:00 P.M. (last day 10:00 A.M.–5:00 P.M.)

RAINY WEATHER: Held indoors   VENDORS: 150   ESTABLISHED: 1991

GETTING THERE: From the South Exit of Niigata Station take bus to Sonoki New Town (曾野木ニュータウン). Get off at stop called Niigata-chiiki Sangyō Shinkō

Center-mae (新潟地域産業振興センター前).

ADDRESS: Niigata-chiiki Sangyō Shinkō Center, 185–10 Shumoku, Niigata-shi, Niigata　新潟県新潟市鐘木185–10　新潟地域産業振興センター

CONTACT: 03–5996–4105, 025–283–1100 (Niigata-chiiki Sangyō Shinkō Center)

Nagano

88. Karuizawa Natsu no Nomi no Ichi　軽井沢 夏の蚤の市

LOCATION: Nagano-ken, Karuizawa-machi, Kyū Karuizawa Kōminkan (旧軽井沢公民館)

NEAREST STATION: Karuizawa (軽井沢), JR Shinetsu Line

WHEN: August 1–31, daily, 9:00 A.M.–7:00 P.M.

RAINY WEATHER: Held indoors　VENDORS: 20　ESTABLISHED: 1966

GETTING THERE: From Karuizawa Station about 10 minutes by car/taxi. Or walk straight north heading toward the Kyū Karuizawa area (Route 133/Kyū-Nakasendō). Turn right on Kankō Kaikan (観光会館) to Karuizawa Tennis Club. Kyū Karuizawa Kōminkan is to the southeast of the tennis club.

ADDRESS: Kyū Karuizawa Kōminkan, 878 Karuizawa-machi, Kita Saku-gun, Nagano
　　　　長野県北佐久郡軽井沢町878　旧軽井沢公民館

CONTACT: 03–5927–4171, 0267–42–2981 (Kyū Karuizawa Kōminkan)

89. Shinshū Kottō Haku　信州 骨董博

LOCATION: Nagano-ken, Matsumoto-shi, Meitetsu Show Hall (名鉄ショーホール)

NEAREST STATION: Matsumoto (松本), JR Chūō Line

WHEN: February or March (3 days), October or November (3 days), 10:00 A.M.–6:00 P.M. (last day, 10:00 A.M.–4:00 P.M.)

RAINY WEATHER: Held indoors　VENDORS: 50　ESTABLISHED: 1989

GETTING THERE: From underground bus terminal at Matsumoto Station take Matsumoto Dentetsu bus line, known as Asahi. Get off at stop called Soyanoguchi (征矢野口).

ADDRESS: Meitetsu Show Hall, 2–8–10 Kamata, Matsumoto-shi, Nagano
　　　　長野県松本市鎌田2–8–10　名鉄ショーホール

CONTACT: 0267–68–2474, 0263–27–4500 (Meitetsu Show Hall)

Shizuoka

90. Mishima Taisha Kottō Matsuri　三嶋大社 骨董まつり

LOCATION: Shizuoka-ken, Mishima-shi, Mishima Taisha Shrine (三嶋大社)

NEAREST STATION: Mishima (三島), JR Tōkaidō Line

WHEN: 4th Saturday, 4th Sunday, 4th Monday; Saturday and Sunday, sunrise–sunset; Monday, sunrise–noon

RAINY WEATHER: Light rain, okay   VENDORS: 15–20   ESTABLISHED: 1998

GETTING THERE: From Mishima Station about 8 minutes by car/taxi.

ADDRESS: Mishima Taisha Shrine, 2–1–5 Ōmiya-chō, Mishima-shi, Shizuoka

静岡県三島市大宮町2-1-5　三嶋大社

CONTACT: 090–3139–4690, 0559–75–0172 (Mishima Shrine)

91. Ogushi Jinja Nomi no Ichi   小梳神社 のみの市

LOCATION: Shizuoka-ken, Shizuoka-shi, Ogushi Shrine (小梳神社)

NEAREST STATION: Shizuoka (静岡) (5 min.), JR Tōkaidō Line

WHEN: 2nd Sunday (in November, changes to 3rd Sunday), 7:00 A.M.–sunset

RAINY WEATHER: Light rain, okay   VENDORS: 40   ESTABLISHED: 1978

GETTING THERE: Walk straight north on Eki-mae Ōdōri. The market is 300 meters down the road on the left.

ADDRESS: Ogushi Shrine, 7–13 Konya-machi, Shizuoka-shi, Shizuoka

静岡県静岡市紺屋町7-13　小梳神社

CONTACT: 0542–53–1478, 054–252–6660 (Ogushi Shrine)

92. Twin Messe Shizuoka, Nagoya Kottō Matsuri
ツインメッセ静岡 名古屋骨董祭

LOCATION: Shizuoka-ken, Shizuoka-shi, Twin Messe Shizuoka (ツインメッセ静岡)

NEAREST STATION: Shizuoka (静岡), JR Tōkaidō Line

WHEN: July (3 days), December (3 days), 9:00 A.M.–5:00 P.M.

RAINY WEATHER: Held indoors   VENDORS: 200   ESTABLISHED: 1995

ENTRANCE FEE: ¥1,000

GETTING THERE: From Shizuoka Station about 7 minutes by car/taxi.

ADDRESS: Twin Messe Shizuoka, 3–1–10, Magarikane, Shizuoka-shi, Shizuoka

静岡県静岡市曲金3-1-10　ツインメッセ静岡

CONTACT: 052–731–5586, 054–285–3111 (Twin Messe Shizuoka)

93. Kottō Festa in Hamamatsu   ザ 骨董フェスタ in 浜松

LOCATION: Shizuoka-ken, Hamamatsu-shi, Act City Hamamatsu (アクトシティ浜松)

NEAREST STATION: Hamamatsu (浜松) (5 min.), JR Tōkaidō Line

WHEN: January 1–3, August 13–15, 10:00 A.M.–6:30 P.M. (last day, noon–6:30 P.M.)

RAINY WEATHER: Held indoors   VENDORS: 90   ESTABLISHED: 1995

GETTING THERE: As you come out the North Exit, turn right. Follow the street that runs along the train tracks for about 300 meters, passing the Okura Hotel, which is in the center of the Act City complex. Act City Event Hall is on the left.

ADDRESS: Act City Hamamatsu, 111–1 Itaya-chō, Hamamatsu-shi, Shizuoka
静岡県浜松市板屋町111-1　アクトシティ浜松
CONTACT: 053–455–3851, 053–451–1111 (Act City Hamamatsu)

Aichi

94. Nagoya Kokusai Antique & Kottō Ichi
名古屋国際アンティック＆骨董市

LOCATION: Aichi-ken, Nagoya-shi, Nagoya Congress Center (Nagoya Kokusai Kaigijō; 名古屋国際会議場)
NEAREST STATION: Hibino (日比野) (5 min.), Meijō subway line
WHEN: April (3 days), November (3 days), 10:00 A.M.–5:00 P.M. (last day, 10:00 A.M.–4:00 P.M.)
RAINY WEATHER: Held indoors   VENDORS: 120   ESTABLISHED: 1998
GETTING THERE: Take Exit 1 and at street level continue walking straight for about 200 meters, then turn right at the signal. The large Nagoya Congress Center hall is on the left.
ADDRESS: Nagoya Kokusai Kaigijō, 1–1 Atsuta Nishi-machi, Atsuta-ku, Nagoya-shi, Aichi　愛知県名古屋市熱田区熱田西町1-1　名古屋国際会議場
CONTACT: 0561–83–8415, 090–1985–5445, 0561–87–1223 (Fax), 052–683–7777 (Nagoya Kokusai Kaigijō)

95. Nagoya Kottō Matsuri   名古屋 骨董祭

LOCATION: Aichi-ken, Nagoya-shi, Chūshō Kigyō Shinkōkaikan, Fukiage Hall (中小企業振興会館吹上ホール)
NEAREST STATION: Fukiage (吹上) (1 min.), Sakura Dōri subway line
WHEN: May (3 days), August (3 days), December (3 days), 9:00 A.M.–5:00 P.M.
RAINY WEATHER: Held indoors   VENDORS: 230   ESTABLISHED: 1991
GETTING THERE: About a 200-meter walk to the west of the station, in Fukiage Park.
ADDRESS: Fukiage Hall, Chūshō Kigyō Shinkōkaikan, 2–6–3 Fukiage, Chigusa-ku, Nagoya-shi, Aichi　愛知県名古屋市千種区吹上2-6-3　中小企業振興会館吹上ホール
CONTACT: 052–731–5586, 052–735–2111 (Fukiage Hall)

96. Ōsu Kannon Kottō Ichi   大須観音 骨董市

LOCATION: Aichi-ken, Nagoya-shi, Ōsu Kannon Temple (大須観音)
NEAREST STATION: Ōsu Kannon (大須観音) (1 min.), Tsurumai subway line
WHEN: 18th of month, 28th of month, sunrise–sunset
RAINY WEATHER: Okay   VENDORS: 80–90   ESTABLISHED: 1980
GETTING THERE: Take the exit signposted Ōsu Kannon Temple. Following any

street running perpendicular to the train tracks, head east for about 50 meters and take the first right. Depending on the street you take, the entrance to the grounds of the temple is 50–250 meters straight ahead.

ADDRESS: Ōsu Kannon Temple, 2–21–47 Ōsu, Naka-ku, Nagoya-shi, Aichi
愛知県名古屋市中区大須2–21–47　大須観音
CONTACT: 052–731–5586, 052–231–6525 (Ōsu Kannon Temple)

Mie

97. **Nandemo Yokka no Ichi**　なんでも四日の市

LOCATION: Mie-ken, Yokka-ichi-shi (near Yokka-ichi City Hall) (市役所近辺)
NEAREST STATION: Yokka-ichi (四日市) (10 min.), JR Kansai/Kintetsu lines
WHEN: Last Sunday (not held in December), 10:00 A.M.–4:00 P.M.
RAINY WEATHER: Okay　VENDORS: 40　ESTABLISHED: 1986
GETTING THERE: Go west for about 500 meters on the wide divided boulevard that runs perpendicular to the train tracks (Chūō Dōri). Turn right at the first major intersection (the city hall is on the corner). The flea market is about 250 meters down at the largish intersection.
ADDRESS: 1–5 Suwa-machi, Yokka-ichi-shi, Mie
三重県四日市市諏訪町1–5
CONTACT: 0593–55–2939

Gifu

98. **Gifu Kottō Matsuri**　岐阜骨董まつり

LOCATION: Gifu-ken, Gifu-shi, Gifu Sangyō Kaikan (岐阜産業会館)
NEAREST STATION: Gifu (岐阜), JR Tōkaidō Line
WHEN: Last Saturday, last Sunday, last Monday (March, September), 10:00 A.M.–5:00 P.M. (last day 10:00 A.M.–4:00 P.M.)
RAINY WEATHER: Held indoors　VENDORS: 70　ESTABLISHED: 1994
GETTING THERE: From Gifu Station take city bus for Kenchō (県庁). Get off at stop called Gifu Sangyō Kaikan-mae (岐阜産業会館前).
ADDRESS: Gifu Sangyō Kaikan, 2–11–1 Rokujo Minami, Gifu-shi, Gifu
岐阜県岐阜市六条南2–11–1　岐阜産業会館
CONTACT: 058–271–3049, 058–272–3921 (Gifu Sangyō Kaikan)

99. **Kogane Jinja Kottō Ichi**　金神社 骨董市

LOCATION: Gifu-ken, Gifu-shi, Kogane Shrine (金神社)
NEAREST STATION: Gifu (岐阜) (5 min.), JR Tōkaidō Line • *Additional station:* Shin-Gifu (新岐阜) (5 min.), Meitetsu Owari Line
WHEN: 9th of month, sunrise–sunset

RAINY WEATHER: Okay   VENDORS: 50–60   ESTABLISHED: 1996

GETTING THERE: From Gifu Station: Walk straight to the north on the main street. The temple is 600 meters down the road on the right.

ADDRESS: Kogane Shrine, 5–3 Kogane-machi, Gifu-shi, Gifu

岐阜県岐阜市金町5–3　金神社

CONTACT: 052–731–5586, 058–262–1316 (Kogane Shrine)

100. Hida Takayama Garakuta Ichi　飛騨高山 我楽多市

LOCATION: Gifu-ken, Takayama-shi, Sanmachi Dōri (三町通り)

NEAREST STATION: Takayama (高山) (10 min.), JR Takayama Line

WHEN: 7th of month (May through October), 9:00 A.M.–5:00 P.M.

RAINY WEATHER: Okay   VENDORS: 20   ESTABLISHED: 1982

GETTING THERE: Take the East Exit, walk west, passing between the bank and Hotel Plaza. Cross the river (about 500 meters down) via the Yanagi-bashi bridge. The market starts 200 meters down the road.

ADDRESS: Sanmachi Dōri, Takayama-shi, Gifu　岐阜県高山市三町通り

CONTACT: 0577–35–3145 (city office)

Toyama

101. Toyama Aozora Nomi no Ichi　富山 青空蚤の市

LOCATION: Toyama-ken, Toyama-shi, Gokoku Shrine (護国神社)

NEAREST STATION: Yasunoya (安野屋) (2 min.), Toyama Chitetsu Line • *Additional station:* Toyama (富山), JR Hokuriku Line

WHEN: 1st Sunday, 5:00 A.M.–3:00 P.M. (April through November), 6:00 A.M.–3:00 P.M. (December through March)

RAINY WEATHER: Okay   VENDORS: 150   ESTABLISHED: 1983

GETTING THERE: From Yasunoya Station: Exit the station and head east, until you get to a river. Just after the river, turn right. Follow the wide street (not the narrow path along the edge of the river) for about 250 meters. The entrance to the grounds of the shrine is straight ahead. From Toyama Station: About 10 minutes by car/taxi.

ADDRESS: Gokoku Shrine, 1–1 Isobe-machi, Toyama-shi, Toyama

富山県富山市磯部町1–1　護国神社

CONTACT: 090–8966–1929, 076–421–6957 (Gokoku Shrine)

Ishikawa

102. Kanazawa Kottō Matsuri　金沢 骨董祭り

LOCATION: Ishikawa-ken, Kanazawa-shi, Ishikawa-ken Sangyō Tenjikan (石川県産業展示館)

NEAREST STATION: Kanazawa (金沢), JR Hokuriku Line

WHEN: Spring (3 days), fall (3 days), 10:00 A.M.–5:00 P.M. (last day 10:00 A.M.–4:00 P.M.)

RAINY WEATHER: Held indoors

VENDORS: 150   **ESTABLISHED:** 1989

GETTING THERE: From Kanazawa Station take the free shuttle bus.

ADDRESS: Ishikawa-ken Sangyō Tenjikan, 193 Minami, Fukurobatake-machi, Kanazawa-shi, Ishikawa　石川県金沢市袋畠町南193　石川県産業展示館

CONTACT: 0762–21–1879, 076–268–1121 (Sangyō Tenjikan)

Fukui

103. **Echizen Kottō Matsuri**　越前 骨董まつり

LOCATION: Fukui-ken, Fukui-shi, Fukui-ken Sangyō Kaikan (福井県産業会館)

NEAREST STATION: Fukui (福井), JR Hokuriku Line

WHEN: January (4 days around New Year's), August (4 days around Obon), 10:00 A.M.–5:00 P.M. (last day 10:00 A.M.–3:00 P.M.)

RAINY WEATHER: Held indoors

VENDORS: 100   **ESTABLISHED:** 1998

GETTING THERE: From Fukui Station take Keifuku bus for Usui Kōkō (羽水高校). Get off at Sangyō Kaikan-mae (産業会館前) bus stop. The ride takes 15 to 20 minutes. Buses leave every 20 to 30 minutes.

ADDRESS: Fukui-ken Sangyō Kaikan, 103 Shimo Rokujō-machi, Fukui-shi, Fukui　福井県福井市下六条町103　福井県産業会館

CONTACT: 0778–52–7039, 0776–41–3611 (Sangyō Kaikan)

SOUTHERN AREA

Hiroshima

104. **Hakushima Nomi no Ichi**　白島 のみの市

LOCATION: Hiroshima-ken, Hiroshima-shi, NTT Kuredo Hakushima (NTTクレド白島)

NEAREST STATION: Hiroshima (広島) (12 min.), JR Sanyō Line

WHEN: 3rd Sunday, 8:00 A.M.–3:00 P.M.

RAINY WEATHER: Okay   **VENDORS:** 20   **ESTABLISHED:** 1995

GETTING THERE: Go out the Omote Exit (South Exit), turn right on Jōhoku Dōri (城北通り), walk along the Kyōbashigawa river (京橋川) past the Tokiwa bridge (常磐橋) and Hakushima intersection. The NTT building is the large structure on right side.

ADDRESS: NTT Kuredo Hakushima, 14–15 Higashi-Hakushima-chō, Naka-ku, Hiroshima-shi, Hiroshima

広島県広島市中区東白島町14–15 NTTクレド白島

CONTACT: 082–888–0355, 082–222–9550 (NTT Kuredo Hakushima)

105. Kottō & Antique in Hiroshima
骨董&アンティック in 広島

LOCATION: Hiroshima-ken, Hiroshima-shi, Hiroshima-shi Chūshō Kigyō Kaikan (広島市中小企業会館)

NEAREST STATION: Shin-Inokuchi (新井口) (15 min.), JR Sanyō Line

WHEN: March (3 days), November (3 days), 10:00 A.M.–5:30 P.M. (last day, 10:00 A.M.–5:00 P.M.)

RAINY WEATHER: Held indoors   VENDORS: 120   ESTABLISHED: 1995

GETTING THERE: Exit the station, walk to the southwest on the main road for about 700 meters. Chūshō Kigyō Kaikan is on the left on the far side of the intersection.

ADDRESS: Hiroshima-shi Chūshō Kigyō Kaikan, 1–14–1 Shōkō Center, Nishi-ku, Hiroshima-shi, Hiroshima

広島県広島市西区商工センター1–14–1 広島市中小企業会館

CONTACT: 082–228–5442 (organizer), 082–277–4441 (Chūshō Kigyō Kaikan)

106. Sumiyoshi Square Kottō Ichi   住吉スクエア骨董市

LOCATION: Hiroshima-ken, Fukuyama-shi, Sumiyoshi Square (住吉スクエア)

NEAREST STATION: Fukuyama (福山) (15 min.), JR Sanyō Line

WHEN: 4th Sunday, sunrise–3:00 P.M.

RAINY WEATHER: Okay   VENDORS: 35–40   ESTABLISHED: 1980

GETTING THERE: Exit the station, walk straight to the city office (about 500 meters), then turn left for another 500 meters. The market is on the right after the intersection.

ADDRESS: Sumiyoshi Square, 1–40 Sumiyoshi-machi, Fukuyama-shi, Hiroshima

広島県福山市住吉町1–40 住吉スクエア

CONTACT: 0849–31–5931, 0849–31–5330 (Sumiyoshi Square)

Yamaguchi

107. Yamaguchi Flea Market Kottō Ichi
山口フリーマーケット骨董市

LOCATION: Yamaguchi-ken, Yamaguchi-shi, Kameyama Park Fureai Hiroba (亀山公園ふれあい広場)

NEAREST STATION: Yamaguchi (山口) (15 min.), JR Yamaguchi Line

WHEN: 1st Sunday, sunrise–3:00 P.M.

RAINY WEATHER: Okay

VENDORS: 300 (about two-thirds of the vendors sell everyday merchandise, not antiques)

ESTABLISHED: 1988

GETTING THERE: Take the exit signposted Kameyama Park. Almost due west of the station, find the street running perpendicular to the train tracks. Heading northwest, follow this street for about 1 kilometer, staying to the right where it forks, until you see the park on your left.

ADDRESS: Kameyama Kōen (Park), Kameyama-machi/Nakagawara-machi, Yamaguchi-shi, Yamaguchi　山口県山口市亀山町～中河原町　亀山公園

CONTACT: 083–927–5599

Fukuoka

108. **Dazaifu Tenjin Omoshiro Ichi**
太宰府天神 おもしろ市

LOCATION: Fukuoka-ken, Dazaifu-shi, Dazaifu Tenmangū Shrine (太宰府天満宮)

NEAREST STATION: Dazaifu (太宰府) (5 min.), Nishitetsu Dazaifu Line

WHEN: March (2 days), May (2 days), July (2 days), September (2 days), October (2 days), December (2 days), sunrise–sunset

RAINY WEATHER: Okay　**VENDORS:** 110　**ESTABLISHED:** 1990

GETTING THERE: 200 meters northeast of the station.

ADDRESS: Dazaifu Tenmangū Shrine, 4–7–1 Zaifu, Dazaifu-shi, Fukuoka
　　　　　福岡県太宰府市宰府4–7–1　太宰府天満宮

CONTACT: 092–922–9955 (tape information), 092–922–8225 (Dazaifu Tenmangū Shrine)

109. **Kottō & Antique in Fukuoka**
骨董＆アンティック in 福岡

LOCATION: Fukuoka-ken, Fukuoka-shi, Kyūden Kinen Tai-ikukan (九電記念体育館)

NEAREST STATION: Hakata (博多), JR Kagoshima/JR Sanyō Shinkansen lines

WHEN: May (3 days), September (3 days), 9:30 A.M.–5:00 P.M.

RAINY WEATHER: Held indoors　**VENDORS:** 90　**ESTABLISHED:** 1999

GETTING THERE: From Hakata Station take Nishitetsu bus no. 9–19. Get off at stop called Minami-Yakuin (南薬院), around 200 meters south.

ADDRESS: Kyūden Kinen Taiikukan, 4–14–1 Yakuin, Chūō-ku, Fukuoka-shi, Fukuoka　福岡県福岡市中央区薬院4–14–1　九電記念体育館

CONTACT: 092–414–8220, 092–531–6961 (Kyūden Kinen Tai-ikukan)

110. **Aya Shusen no Mori Kottō Nomi no Ichi**
綾　酒泉の杜 骨董のみの市

LOCATION: Miyazaki-ken, Aya-shi, Aya Shusen no Mori (綾・酒泉の杜)
NEAREST STATION: Minami Miyazaki (南宮崎), JR Nippō Line
WHEN: March (2 days), September (2 days), 8:00 A.M.–5:00 P.M.
RAINY WEATHER: Held indoors   VENDORS: 60   ESTABLISHED: 1987
GETTING THERE: From Minami Miyazaki Station take bus bound for Shusen no Mori.
ADDRESS: Aya Shusen no Mori, Minami Mata, Aya-chō, Higashi Morokata-gun,
Miyazaki　宮崎県東諸県郡綾町南俣　綾・酒泉の杜
CONTACT: 0985–77–3611, 0985–77–2222 (Shusen no Mori)

Miyazaki

111. **Kottō Nomi no Ichi Matsuri in Miyazaki**
骨董蚤の市まつり in 宮崎

LOCATION: Miyazaki-ken, Miyazaki-shi, JA Azumu Hall (JAアズムホール)
NEAREST STATION: Miyazaki (宮崎) (10 min.), JR Nippō Line
WHEN: January (2 days), March (2 days), July (2 days), November (2 days), 8:30
A.M.–5:30 P.M.
RAINY WEATHER: Held indoors   VENDORS: 30   ESTABLISHED: 1993
GETTING THERE: Take the West Exit and head west toward Miyazaki Ōhashi bridge
(宮崎大橋). Turn right after Miyazaki Hospital (about 1.5 kilometers down), and
walk about another kilometer. JA Azumu Hall is on the left.
ADDRESS: JA Azumu Hall, 1–1–1 Kirishima, Miyazaki-shi, Miyazaki
　　　　　宮崎県宮崎市霧島1–1–1　JAアズムホール
CONTACT: 099–260–3719, 0985–31–2202 (JA Azumu Hall)

Kagoshima

112. **Kyūshū Kottō Matsuri**　九州骨董祭り

LOCATION: Kagoshima-ken, Kagoshima-shi, Sky Road Mizobe (スカイロードみ
ぞべ)
WHEN: 4th Saturday, 4th Sunday, odd-numbered months (Jan., Mar., May, July,
Sept., Nov.), 8:00 A.M.–5:00 P.M.
RAINY WEATHER: Okay (held under tent)   VENDORS: 40   ESTABLISHED: 1998
GETTING THERE: From Kagoshima Airport about 3 minutes by car/taxi, near the
north end of landing strip, on the left side of Route 504.
ADDRESS: Sky Road Mizobe, 2399 Mizobe-chō, Aira-gun, Kagoshima
　　　　　鹿児島県姶良郡溝辺町2399　スカイロードみぞべ
CONTACT: 0995–47–0181

113. Satsuma Nana-ju-nana-man-goku Kottō Matsuri
薩摩七十七萬石 骨董祭り

LOCATION: Kagoshima-ken, Kagoshima-shi, Oroshi Danchi Kumiai Kaikan (卸団地組合会館)

NEAREST STATION: Nishi-Kagoshima (西鹿児島), JR Kagoshima Line

WHEN: 8:30 A.M.–6:00 P.M., 5 to 6 times a year (2 days each)

RAINY WEATHER: Held indoors VENDORS: 40 ESTABLISHED: 1998

GETTING THERE: Take the street car (*shiden*) to Tanimachi Station, then take a taxi for a 30-minute ride. The street car runs approximately once an hour.

ADDRESS: Oroshi Danchi Kumiai Kaikan, 6–12 Oroshi Hon-chō, Kagoshima-shi, Kagoshima 鹿児島県鹿児島市卸本町6–12 卸団地組合会館

CONTACT: 099–260–3719

114. Terukuni Jinja Nomi no Ichi 照国神社 のみの市

LOCATION: Kagoshima-ken, Kagoshima-shi, Terukuni Shrine (照国神社)

NEAREST STATION: Tenmonkan (天文館) (10 min.), Shiden Line

WHEN: February (3 days), 7:00 A.M.–5:00 P.M.

RAINY WEATHER: Okay VENDORS: 35 ESTABLISHED: 2001

GETTING THERE: Take the exit signposted Terukuni Shrine. About 100 meters west of the station, find the street running perpendicular to the train tracks. Heading northwest, follow this street for about 400 meters, until you reach a T-junction. Turn left at the T-junction, go about 50 meters, then turn right. The entrance to the grounds of the shrine is about 250 meters straight ahead.

ADDRESS: Terukuni Shrine, 19–35 Terukuni-chō, Kagoshima-shi, Kagoshima
　　　　　　鹿児島県鹿児島市照国町19–35 照国神社

CONTACT: 0995–47–0181, 099–222–1820 (Terukuni Shrine)

Kagawa

115. Chūgoku Shikoku Kottōhin Tenji Sokubaikai, Sanuki Kottō Ichi 中国四国 骨董品展示即売会 さぬき骨董市

LOCATION: Kagawa-ken, Takamatsu-shi, Sun Messe Kagawa (サンメッセ香川)

NEAREST STATION: Takamatsu (高松), JR Yosan Line

WHEN: February (3 days), June (3 days), November (3 days), 10:00 A.M.–5:00 P.M.

RAINY WEATHER: Held indoors VENDORS: 150–200 ESTABLISHED: 1992

GETTING THERE: From Takamatsu Station take bus no. 8 bound for Sun Messe Kagawa (takes 30 minutes).

ADDRESS: Sun Messe Kagawa, 2217-1 Hayashi-machi, Takamatsu-shi, Kagawa
　　　　　　香川県高松市林町2217–1 サンメッセ香川

CONTACT: 087–749–4838, 087–869–3333 (Sun Messe Kagawa)

IV. THINGS TO BUY

At any given point in time, there is no telling what kind of wonderful old stuff might emerge from Japan's houses, temples, offices, factories, barns, warehouses, and workshops. But you can bet that much of what surfaces, if it has any resale value, is going to find its way to a flea market.

The variety of merchandise turning up at flea markets is quite amazing: ceramics, textiles, furniture, religious and ceremonial objects, clothing, toys, games, flags, banners, weapons, kitchen utensils, tools, and farming implements. And this is just the beginning.

The purpose of this section is to help the foreign flea-market shopper make sense of it all. It is a daunting task—indeed, some items are so old or obsolete that modern Japanese, sometimes even the people selling them, are hard-pressed to explain what they were used for. But the names and definitions included here—almost 450 of them—will get you started.

While that is a lot of entries, it is impossible to cover everything, as the number of items on sale at flea markets is not only too numerous but also too random and unpredictable. However, most of the items that can be considered representative or typical, those that appear the most regularly, are included.

The antiques, artifacts, and assorted other merchandise to be found are conveniently classified into 18 categories—such as Ceramics, Textiles, and Lacquerware—with items listed separately in an alphabetical index to facilitate quick and easy usage.

To make it easier to recognize some of the merchandise, the section also includes photographs and illustrations of many of the more popular items for sale. If your command of Japanese is limited, at least you can point to one of these pictures.

NOTE: The names of items are shown without the honorific prefix (*o-* or *go-*) except where the prefix has become for all intents and purposes part of the name itself. In such cases, dropping it would sound strange and perhaps cause confusion. Thus, *o-hajiki* (the glass or ceramic pieces used in a game similar to marbles) is always *o-hajiki* and never simply *hajiki*. In most cases the prefix is optional, but adding it sounds more polite. This is why *sara* (plate or dish), to give just one example, sometimes becomes *o-sara*.

ARCHITECTURAL ARTIFACTS

This category is young, both in the sense that it has developed quite recently and that many of the items are not particularly old. The merchandise, however, is deceiving in that it tends to look and feel old, either because it has been used extensively or exposed for years to the elements. That it has acquired a patina explains much of its appeal. Dealers bring to market pieces of large structures or objects—a board, a beam, a section of a ladder, a segment of a fence—since just about anything with character will sell.

Some items in this category would be difficult to display, but almost all of them can be put to use in an architectural setting or incorporated into the structure of a modern house or apartment. For example, as part of a bathroom renovation, a stone basin could be turned into a sink, while a sliding door could be used as, well, a door, but of the swinging variety with a handle attached.

This category is organized into two sections, Exterior and Interior. The Exterior section includes a few items used in the traditional Japanese landscape garden.

EXTERIOR

amado　雨戸 (あまど) removable sliding wooden shutters

fumi-ishi　踏み石 (ふみいし)

    block of stone used as a step to enter a traditional Japanese house from the garden or interior work area (*doma*)

fūtaku　風鐸 (ふうたく)

    chain used in lieu of vertical drainpipe in a shrine; water from the gutter trickles down the chain to the ground

hashigo　梯子 (はしご)

    ladder; may be used in lieu of stairway in barn, stable, or traditional house

hyōsatsu　表札 (ひょうさつ)

    nameplate or doorplate found on, beside, or above the entrance to a house or temple

ishidōrō　石灯籠 (いしどうろう)

    stone lantern found in traditional Japanese gardens; nowadays acts as an aesthetic element, no longer serving its original purpose of lighting a path or the edge of a pond

kawara　瓦 (かわら)

    roof tiles (usually gray, sometimes brown) used on traditional Japanese buildings; most are flat or slightly curved; eave or roof-ridge tiles are often shaped like demons or fish

kōshido　格子戸 (こうしど)

    sliding wooden latticework doors, similar to *shōji* but with heavier frame and without paper; used as gate at exterior of grounds of Japanese house

sudare　簾 (すだれ)

    screen made from strips of bamboo, reeds, or hemp stalks, hung from the edge of an eve or used to cover a window; rolled up and down like a vertical blind

tobira/to　扉 (とびら)/戸 (と)

    door of a house or building

door handle

tsukubai　蹲 (つくばい)

    stone basin found in traditional Japanese gardens; its original function was to hold water for hand washing before taking part in the tea ceremony

tsuri-dōrō　釣り灯籠 (つりどうろう)

hanging metal lantern found on the grounds of a temple; originally illuminated by a candle or oil-burning lamp

yoshizu　葦簀 (よしず)

large portable reed screen used to protect the façade of a home or shop front from the sun

INTERIOR

fusuma　襖 (ふすま)

sliding door made by covering both sides of a light wooden frame with thick paper; often decorated with paintings or colored paper

ranma　欄間 (らんま)

decorative wooden panel placed above a door or window; features relief carving or openwork designs

ranma

shōji　障子 (しょうじ)

sliding door made by covering one side of a light wooden grid with translucent white paper

sudo/natsudo　簾戸 (すど)/夏戸 (なつど)

sliding door made of slatted wood, reed or a bamboo screen within a wooden frame, used instead of *shōji* or *fusuma* in summer; by allowing air to pass through, it helps keep house cool

BASKETS, BOXES, BUCKETS, AND BARRELS

This category is notable for the large number of everyday items that it contains, most oozing with character. Their character comes from the natural materials of which they are made—usually bamboo and wood, which tend to improve with age—and from the many hours of use they have received, which gives them a well-used, antique look, even if they don't happen to be particularly old.

Because these are everyday objects, they are almost never pretentious, and this directness and honesty adds to their appeal. The craftsmanship is often excellent. Japanese box making and cooperage rank among some of the world's best.

BASKETS

biku 魚籠 (びく) fisherman's creel, or basket used for holding fish

hana kago 花籠 (はなかご)
basket used for flower arrangement

kago 籠 (かご) basket

kusakari kago 草刈籠 (くさかりかご)
basket used to hold leaves and grass clippings; sometimes used for compost

mi 箕 (み) winnowing basket

mi

mondori もんどり
fish trap baited and submerged in shallow water

mondori
and biku

seoi kago/shoi kago
背負い籠 (せおいかご/しょいかご)
harvest and general carrying basket, worn strapped to the back; the straps are often decoratively woven with colorful fabric and rice straw

tekago 手籠 (てかご) hand basket

torikago 鳥籠 (とりかご) birdcage

seoi kago

warada　わらだ

>flat silkworm-breeding basket used to hold silkworms and the mulberry leaves on which they feed; round or rectangular

zaru　笊（ざる）shallow basket, basket sieve

BOXES

dōgu-bako　道具箱（どうぐばこ）tool box

fumi-bako　文箱（ふみばこ）

>box used to hand-deliver letters, passed back and forth between correspondents

hako　箱（はこ）box

hitsu　櫃（ひつ）

>wooden box or crate; usually used to store grain

jū-bako　重箱（じゅうばこ）

>tiered, stackable food boxes; lacquerware or ceramic

kami-bako　紙箱（かみばこ）box made of paper

kamiyui no dōguire　髪結いの道具入れ（かみゆいのどうぐいれ）

>wooden box used by hair dresser to hold combs, hair pins, and other accessories

keshō-bako　化粧箱（けしょうばこ）

>container for cosmetics or makeup

kusuri-bako　薬箱（くすりばこ）medicine box

hako

kusuri-bako

mage-mono / mage-wappa 曲げ物（まげもの）/
曲げわっぱ（まげわっぱ）

bentwood container, most often a *bentō* (packed or picnic lunch) box; commonly made of a coniferous wood and often fastened with strips of cherry bark

mochi-bako 餅箱（もちばこ）

shallow rectangular box without top used for carrying *mochi* (rice cakes)

suzuri-bako 硯箱（すずりばこ）

writing box (holds ink, inkstone, water dropper, and brush); usually lacquerware

toro-bako とろ箱（とろばこ）

shallow rectangular box without top used for carrying fish

BUCKETS AND BARRELS

oke 桶（おけ）
wooden bucket, pail, tub (often with a handle)

oke

taga 箍（たが）

tight-fitting band, made of either interwoven strips of bamboo or copper, that holds together the staves of a bucket, tub, etc.

taru 樽（たる）wooden barrel, keg

tsurube つるべ

wooden bucket used to scoop water out of a well

CERAMICS

Ceramics is one of the most highly developed Japanese crafts, and one of the most popular types of merchandise for sale at flea markets today. There are a number of reasons for this. Cups, bowls, plates, and other types of tableware are attractive enough to display yet sturdy enough to use every day. Because there are many in circulation and they tend to come in sets, they make ideal collectibles. Finally, the sheer variety of items available, even within the narrow range of Japanese blue-and-white porcelain, means there is something for practically everyone.

This section is divided into three categories—ceramic forms, porcelain, and stoneware.

CERAMIC FORMS

abura tsubo　油壺 (あぶらつぼ) oil bottle

binbō-dokkuri　びんぼう徳利 (びんぼうどっくり)
　　large ceramic saké bottle

chataku　茶托 (ちゃたく)
　　Japanese-style saucer; made of wood, lacquerware, or metal

chiri-renge　ちりれんげ
　　Chinese-style spoon, usually porcelain

choku / choko / guinomi　猪口 (ちょく/ちょこ)/ ぐいのみ
　　saké cup; *guinomi* is larger than *choku/choko*

chōshi　銚子 (ちょうし) saké pot

dobin　土瓶 (どびん) large teapot

donburi　丼 (どんぶり)
　　large, deep bowl used for rice or noodle dishes

funa-dokkuri　船徳利 (ふなどっくり)
　　large ceramic bottle used on a ship; broad base and low center of gravity for stability; used for saké, oil, and other liquids

futa　蓋 (ふた) lid, cover, or cap

hachi　鉢 (はち) medium- to large-sized bowl

haidai　盃台 (はいだい) saké-cup rest

haizara　灰皿 (はいざら) ashtray

haniwa　埴輪 (はにわ)
　　tomb figures, made from about A.D. 400 to 650; inexpensive copies
　　often appear at flea markets

hashi-oki　箸置き (はしおき) chopstick rest

hibachi　火鉢 (ひばち)
　　charcoal brazier for warming the hands

kabin/hana ire/kaki　花瓶 (かびん)/花入れ (はないれ)/花器 (かき)
　　vase; vessel for flower arrangement

kame　瓶 (かめ) very large jar or storage vessel

kōgō　香合 (こうごう) incense box, incense container

kōro　香炉 (こうろ) incense burner

kōtate　香立て (こうたて)
　　incense burner with holes to hold sticks of incense

kyūsu　急須 (きゅうす) small teapot

meimei-zara　銘々皿 (めいめいざら)
　　saucer-sized set of dishes/plates

ōzara　大皿 (おおざら) large platter

rōsoku-tate　蝋燭立て (ろうそくたて) candle-
　　holder

sara　皿 (さら) plate or flat dish

soba choko　そば猪口 (そばちょこ)
　　cup to hold sauce into which *soba* (buckwheat
　　noodles) are dipped

soba choko

tokkuri　徳利 (とっくり) saké flask, saké bottle

tsubo　壺 (つぼ) jar, storage jar, or crock

ueki-bachi　植木鉢 (うえきばち) flowerpot

tokkuri

Arita-yaki　有田焼 （ありたやき）

porcelain wares made in the Arita area of
northern Kyūshū from the 17th century
onwards; most commonly, blue on white

beniguchi　紅口 （べにぐち）

porcelain plate, dish, or bowl, usually
blue-and-white, with a brown rim or edge

Imari　伊万里 （いまり）

Arita-yaki

popular name for Arita-yaki, taken from the
name of the port in Kyūshū from which the porcelain was shipped

Ko Imari　古伊万里 （こいまり）

Old Imari, produced from about 1650 to 1750; moderately rare, expensive

Shoki Imari　初期伊万里 （しょきいまり）

Early Imari, produced from 1616 to 1650; extremely rare, very expensive

Imari   Ko Imari

Kakiemon　柿右衛門 （かきえもん）

overglaze-enameled porcelain produced in the Arita area, famous for
its red enamel color and light decoration

Kutani-yaki　九谷焼 （くたにやき）

type of porcelain made in Ishikawa Prefecture; generally characterized
by bold overglaze-enamel designs using a palette of five colors (red,
green, blue, yellow, and purple)

Nabeshima　鍋島 （なべしま）

porcelain characterized by its understated elegance and exquisite
artistry; now much copied or emulated as a "style"

sometsuke　染付け （そめつけ）

blue-and-white porcelain decorated with cobalt underglaze

CERAMICS

STONEWARE (TŌKI)

Bizen-yaki　備前焼 （びぜんやき）

unglazed stoneware of Okayama Prefecture; characterized by earthy shades, from iron red through dark brown

Hagi-yaki　萩焼き （はぎやき）

pottery from the town of Hagi in Yamaguchi Prefecture mainly used for the tea ceremony; characterized by delicate glaze color that changes with years of use

Karatsu-yaki　唐津焼 （からつやき）

tea-ceremony ware generally characterized by iron underglaze decoration under an ash glaze; made in the town of Karatsu in Saga Prefecture

Karatsu-yaki

Kyō-yaki　京焼き （きょうやき）

collective name for a range of porcelain, stoneware, raku ware, and low-fired overglaze-enamel wares produced in Kyoto; characterized by detailed, ornate designs incorporating a wide variety of motifs and colors; much of the production is for the tea ceremony and flower arrangement

Mashiko-yaki / Kasama-yaki　益子焼 （ましこやき）/ 笠間焼き （かさまやき）

glazed stoneware made in the towns of Mashiko and Kasama in Tochigi Prefecture; generally characterized by simple linear or geometric designs in black, brown, and beige

Mashiko-yaki

Mino　美濃 （みの）

a general term for ceramics produced in the Mino area, in Gifu Prefecture, including Oribe, Shino, and Seto ware.

Onta-yaki / Koishibara

小鹿田焼き （おんたやき）/ 小石原 （こいしばら）

pottery of folk kilns of northern Kyūshū; known for splashed glaze, chattermark, and brushmark pattern decorations

Oribe　織部 （おりべ）

pottery characterized by free decoration in underglaze iron and areas of green glaze against a beige ground; named after tea master Furuta Oribe

Oribe

Satsuma　薩摩 （さつま）

folk pottery made by lineages of Korean potters who settled in Kagoshima in the 17th century; comes in black and white varieties

Seto　瀬戸 （せと）

refers to a wide range of stoneware and porcelain, mainly everyday household and restaurant crockery; varieties include green-on-yellow (*ki-seto*) and black (*seto-guro*)

Seto

Shino　志野 （しの）

varieties of stoneware exhibiting a thick feldspar glaze and underglaze iron decoration

Shino

yakishime　焼きしめ （やきしめ）

unglazed stoneware, mainly pots for farm and household use; decorative effects are produced by accidental events in the kiln firing (known as *yōhen*)

COMMERCIAL ART AND ADVERTISING

In an earlier era, advertising and commercial art—products ranging from gilded wooden shop signs to painted metal signs to package labels—embraced the crass, the cute, and the classy, in an all-out attempt to get noticed. Whether refined or showy, this category has lots of potential for anyone who enjoys what it offers in terms of aesthetics, and appreciates what it offers as an expression of pop culture.

Because many items were mass-produced, they are relatively easy to find and, except for old wooden store signs (*ita kanban*), very affordably priced.

banzuke　番付（ばんづけ）
> chart showing sumo tournament match-ups

chirashi　ちらし　flyer, leaflet, brochure

eiga no posutā　映画のポスター
> movie poster; posters advertising romantic comedies, gangster films, and samurai flicks are the most common

hōrō kanban　琺瑯看板（ホーローかんばん）
> painted metal outdoor sign

ita kanban　板看板（いたかんばん）
> wooden store or product sign; usually made from a single piece of wood, with carved and painted text and graphical elements

hōrō kanban　　　　ita kanban

posutā　ポスター　poster

shīru/raberu　シール/ラベル
> seal, label; sometimes sold in the form of a large sheet of paper with many copies of a label printed on it

DOLLS, PUPPETS, GAMES, AND TOYS

Antique dolls, puppets, games, and toys provide a fascinating glimpse into the leisure and recreation activities of an earlier era. It is unusual for some of these items to show up at flea markets, and when they do they are often in poor condition. Yet even the dilapidated items have display potential.

Nontraditional items are not included here. However, this category contains many items that, although traditional, are not antique. Most of the games for adults, such as mah-jongg, *shōgi* and *go*, are still played widely. Most of the dolls, popular as souvenirs, are still made in large quantities. Naturally such contemporary items tend to be in better condition.

It is important to mention that many of the most avid collectors of items in this category, extended to include modern toys such as trains, robots, race cars, and stuffed animals, attend toy shows or specialized swap meets organized separately from antique markets. That such events take place is no doubt one of the reasons the supply of these items at flea markets is limited.

DOLLS AND PUPPETS

gogatsu ningyō　五月人形（ごがつにんぎょう）
> doll set for Boy's Day (now called Children's Day) centering around a boy warrior with a miniature set of samurai armor and other accessories

Hakata ningyō　博多人形（はかたにんぎょう）
> small colorful folk figurine made of molded clay; produced in the Hakata area of Fukuoka Prefecture

hariko　張り子（はりこ）
> papier-mâché; also refers to a small painted papier-mâché doll, usually a Miharu *ningyō*

hina ningyō / o-hina-sama
　雛人形（ひなにんぎょう）/ **お雛さま**（おひなさま）
> doll set for the Hina Festival (now called the Doll Festival) featuring a member of the imperial court on a raised platform along with lacquerware accessories and other traditional items reproduced in miniature

kimekomi ningyō　木目込み人形（きめこみにんぎょう）
> so-called Edo art doll; the body is made of molded wood composite, which is painted to accent facial and other features; clothing and hair

is attached by tucking into grooves cut into the body

kokeshi こけし

cylindrical wooden doll made on a lathe, with painted folk designs; produced in northern Honshu

Miharu ningyō 三春人形 (みはるにんぎょう)

colorful papier-mâché folk figurines made in Fukushima Prefecture

kimekomi ningyō

ningyō 人形 (にんぎょう)

generic term for doll or puppet

kokeshi

GAMES AND TOYS

go 碁 (ご)

strategic board game; playing set consists of black (slate) and white (shell) "stones" plus a large wooden board

gunjin shōgi 軍人将棋 (ぐんじんしょうぎ)

a military board game related to *shōgi* only in name; wooden pieces represent personnel of different ranks and equipment of different strengths

hagoita 羽子板 (はごいた)

referred to as a battledore, this is a sort of paddle used to hit a shuttle-cock (similar to a badminton birdy) in the traditional New Year's game *hanetsuki*; today the game is rarely played, but elaborate, decorated *hagoita*, with padded silk relief work of kabuki actors and modern celebrities, are sold at the year-end

hanafuda 花札 (はなふだ)

traditional Japanese playing cards, printed on one side with flower designs; the deck contains 48 cards, divided into 12 sets of 4; each set corresponds to a month of the year

kami-shibai 紙芝居 (かみしばい)

picture-card show; in this pre-TV form of children's entertainment, a showman would tell a story based on a series of images drawn on large pieces of cardboard

hagoita

hanafuda

karuta　歌留多（かるた）

generic term for traditional Japanese playing cards of all kinds

karuta

koma　独楽（こま）

tops made of various materials; once popular with small boys for "top wars"

mājan　麻雀（マージャン）

mah-jongg

menko　面子（めんこ）

a game played only by boys in which two or more players attempt to collect as many of the opponent's illustrated cardboard cards as possible

o-hajiki　おはじき

roughly equivalent to marbles, a game played mostly by girls; uses colorful little glass disks

shōgi　将棋（しょうぎ）

Japanese chess; roughly equivalent to Western chess

sugoroku　双六（すごろく）

generic term for board game involving the moving of counters toward a goal by the throw of dice

FARMING IMPLEMENTS AND TOOLS

Farming implements and tools have started to appear at flea markets in the last few years and are beginning to gain in popularity, to the point that some vendors now specialize in them. These utilitarian objects may not qualify as Art with a capital A, but some display the artistry of the master craftsman, and many are undeniably beautiful, though they were not designed as decorative items. Moreover, compared to items of less humble origins, they are very affordable.

FARMING IMPLEMENTS

kama 鎌（かま）sickle

kumade 熊手（くまで）rake

kura 鞍（くら）saddle

kuwa 鍬（くわ）hoe, mattock

sori 橇（そり）sled, sleigh

suki 犂（すき）plow

suki / shaberu / sukoppu
鋤（すき）/シャベル/スコップ　shovel

yuki kaki 雪かき（ゆきかき）snow shovel

kura

suki

TOOLS

chōna 手斧（ちょうな）adz

ito-guruma 糸車（いとぐるま）
spinning wheel

ito-maki 糸巻き（いとまき）
spool, bobbin

kanazuchi 金槌（かなづち）hammer

kanna 鉋（かんな）plane, draw shave

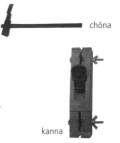

chōna

kanna

kebiki 罫引き（けびき）

marking gauge (tool used to score a line on a board before sawing it)

kinuta 砧（きぬた）

wooden mallet used in fabric-making process

kizuchi 木槌（きづち）

wooden mallet

kote 鏝（こて） trowel, smoothing iron

nata 鉈（なた） Japanese hatchet

nokogiri 鋸（のこぎり） saw

nomi 鑿（のみ） chisel

ono 斧（おの） ax

nokogiri

sumi-tsubo 墨壷（すみつぼ）

ink line (like a Western chalk line, but black); often comes in an ornately carved container

tekagi 手鈎（てかぎ）

short pole with a hook on the end; used to grab hold of shipping crates or other cargo

yagen 薬研（やげん）

druggist's mortar, used to grind herbs and roots into powder; consists of a sharp-edged wheel with handles on either side and a base with a rut or groove into which the wheel fits

yakigote 焼き鏝（やきこて）

tool similar to branding iron; used to imprint wooden objects with family crest or other identifying mark

yattoko/penchi やっとこ/ペンチ

pliers or pincers

yattoko / penchi

FLAGS AND BANNERS

Flags and banners are some of the rarest finds at flea markets, but are usually worth hunting for. Aside from their novelty appeal, their big, bold designs; bright colors; and generous dimensions are visually arresting. A typical fishing-boat banner could attractively fill the wall of an average-sized Western living room.

A flag or banner could also be displayed outside, flown from a flagpole, hung from the railing of a front porch, or suspended vertically below a second-story window; after all, these items were originally intended for outdoor use, and are quite capable of withstanding the elements.

fukinagashi　吹き流し（ふきながし）
> set of multicolored streamers flown above *koinobori*

gunki　軍旗（ぐんき）
> military flag

koinobori　鯉幟り（こいのぼり）
> wind-sock banner in the form
> of a carp (*koi*); flown before and
> after Children's Day (May 5)

koinobori

maku　幕（まく）
> textile used to delineate a boundary for festivals, funerals, or other kinds of gatherings; any suspended textile used for decorative/ritual purposes, interior or exterior

nobori　幟り（のぼり）
> generic term for traditional banner; it is hung vertically, attached to a pole by loops sewn into one or more edges; used for everything from festivals to used car sales

tairyō-bata/tairyō-ki　大漁旗（たいりょうばた/たいりょうき）
> fishing-boat banner flown on return to port to announce a big catch; still made at some fishing ports

FURNITURE AND FIXTURES

Japanese furniture is not only unique in design but also uniquely beautiful. It is characterized by utilitarian style, with little ornamentation but solid construction. Japanese chests seem to fit into almost any modern interior, which is one reason they are so much in demand. Those with intricately worked iron fittings are now extremely rare and expensive. Other types of furniture familiar in the West were not used in the traditional Japanese house.

Truly high-quality items in this category, not necessarily sold at flea markets, cost a small fortune; and even items of average quality, which are found at flea markets, tend to be pricey.

FURNITURE

chabudai　茶袱台 (ちゃぶだい)
　　　low dining table with foldable legs; stored away when not in use

chadansu　茶箪笥 (ちゃだんす)
　　　cabinet or cupboard for teacups, teapot, and tea-making accoutrements

fude-dansu　筆箪笥 (ふでだんす)
　　　writing chest

fumidai　踏み台 (ふみだい)
　　　stepladder or portable step; used inside the home to access out-of-reach places

funa-dansu　船箪笥 (ふなだんす)
　　　ship chest; usually a strongbox with elaborate hardware

funa-dansu

haribako　針箱 (はりばこ)
　　　traditional sewing box, usually with little drawers and a hinged top

kaidan-dansu　階段箪笥 (かいだんだんす)
　　　multitiered chest of drawers that doubles as a set of steps, used by occupants of a house to ascend to the floor above

kazaridana　飾り棚 (かざりだな)
　　　shelves used in a home to display objects

kaidan-dansu

koshikake　腰掛け（こしかけ）stool

kotatsu　火燵（こたつ）
　foot warmer; a charcoal brazier is placed beneath a wooden frame, and the frame is covered with a quilt

kotatsu yagura　火燵やぐら（こたつやぐら）
　frame of a *kotatsu*

kuruma-dansu　車箪笥（くるまだんす）
　chest mounted on wheels; could be moved easily in and out of a warehouse, could be removed quickly in event of fire

kusuri-dansu　薬箪笥（くすりだんす）
　chest for medicine or herbal remedies; usually has several rows of small drawers or compartments

kyōsoku/hijikake　脇息（きょうそく）/肘掛け（ひじかけ）
　armrest for use by a person sitting on the floor

mizuya-dansu/mizuya　水屋箪笥（みずやだんす）/水屋（みずや）
　kitchen chest

o-tanazukue　御店机（おたなづくえ）
　shopkeeper's desk; long and low-slung, almost like a bench, with a few small drawers; designed for the shopkeeper to sit behind, facing outward toward the customers; the front face often incorporates a sign advertising a brand or product

shōhin-dana　商品棚（しょうひんだな）
　shelves used in a shop to display merchandise

tansu　箪笥（たんす）
　chest, chest of drawers

temoto-dansu　手元箪笥（てもとだんす）
　small set of drawers

terakoya-zukue　寺子屋机（てらこやづくえ）
　small, low desk

zeni-bako　銭箱（ぜにばこ）
　money box; often contains small drawers in addition to main compartment

zeni-bako

andon 行灯 (あんどん)
  candle- or oil-burning lamp; usually made of wood, with sides made of paper

bonbori 雪洞 (ぼんぼり)
  fancy oil or candle lamp; generally consists of a graceful silk or paper shade over a lacquered pedestal

andon

byōbu 屏風 (びょうぶ)
  freestanding, folding screen-partition, usually with designs painted on silk or paper

chōba-gōshi 帳場格子 (ちょうばごうし)
  low wooden latticework partition

chōchin 提灯 (ちょうちん)
  paper lantern

denki-gasa / denki no kasa
  電気傘 (でんきがさ) / 電気の傘 (でんきのかさ)
  light fixture; lampshade

chōchin

Gifu chōchin 岐阜提灯 (ぎふちょうちん)
  graceful silk lantern with painted decoration, used for the Bon Festival; also called Obon *chōchin* (though technically a Gifu *chōchin* is any paper lantern made in the town of Gifu)

hibachi 火鉢 (ひばち)
  container to hold a bed of sand and ashes on which a charcoal fire burns; functions as a handwarmer and source of heat for a kettle; made in various forms, including hollowed out tree sections (see also Ceramics)

kagami 鏡 (かがみ) mirror

kanagu 金具 (かなぐ)
  metal fittings, hardware on furniture

konabachi 粉鉢 (こなばち)
  large wooden bowl for mixing dough, etc.

naga hibachi　長火鉢（ながひばち）
　　a rectangular box-form hibachi

rōsoku-tate　蠟燭立て（ろうそくたて）
　　candleholder

shokudai　燭台（しょくだい）
　　high-class candle or oil lamp

teshoku　手燭（てしょく）
　　hand-held metal candleholder

tokei　時計（とけい）
　　clock, watch

rōsoku-tate

tsuitate　衝立（ついたて）
　　freestanding wooden screen-partition, often with designs carved in relief

KITCHEN UTENSILS

Since cooking takes place in every household, it is probably not surprising that kitchen utensils are sold at flea markets in great numbers. Whether it is a wood-burning stove you are after, a cast-iron kettle, or a mortar and pestle, you are likely to find it.

Displayed—or used—with a little imagination, these fascinating everyday objects can add an element of interest to various contexts.

bon　盆（ぼん）tray

hai narashi　灰均し（はいならし）
　　rake or leveler for hearth and *hibachi* ash

hera　箆（へら）spatula

hibashi　火箸（ひばし）
　　iron chopsticks used to handle coals

hishaku　柄杓（ひしゃく）ladle

jizaikagi 自在鉤 (じざいかぎ)

   pole-and-hook apparatus used to suspend kettle
   or cooking pot above *irori* (sunken open hearth)

kashigata 菓子型 (かしがた)

   wooden mold used to make certain kinds of traditional Japanese confectionery

kibachi 木鉢 (きばち)

   wooden bowl or basin

kine 杵 (きね) pestle, pounder

konro 焜炉 (こんろ)

   portable cooker; traditionally charcoal-
   burning, now fueled by gas or
   kerosene

masu 桝 (ます)

   small, square wooden container used
   as dry or liquid measure

mushiki 蒸し器 (むしき)

   steamer

seiro 蒸篭/蒸籠 (せいろ)

   stackable wooden racks used for steam-cooking

sutōbu ストーブ

   wood- or charcoal-burning cast-iron stove

tetsubin 鉄瓶 (てつびん)

   cast-iron kettle used to heat water for domestic use

usu 臼 (うす)

   large wooden mortar

yakan やかん

   kettle for heating water

yutō 湯桶/湯斗 (ゆとう)

   square or round pitcher that holds cooking water from *soba* (buckwheat) noodles; made of lacquerware or bentwood

o-zen 御膳 (おぜん)

   tray-table; usually made of lacquered wood

jizaikagi

kashigata

tetsubin

LACQUERWARE

Until the mid-1980s, Japanese did not generally buy used lacquerware. Now it is actively sought after and regularly appears at flea markets. Lacquerware bowls and boxes are often sold in complete sets of three, five, or more, although it is quite possible to find attractive one-off items to mix and match.

In most of its varieties, lacquerware is formal and dignified, which makes it suitable for classy settings and special occasions, even if it is purchased secondhand.

gōroku-wan　合鹿椀（ごうろくわん）
　　large, heavy lacquerware food bowl with high foot

itsutsu-wan　五つ椀（いつつわん）
　　nested set of five lacquerware food bowls

negoro　根来（ねごろ）
　　red-on-black lacquerware; the red wears off in places, creating a pleasing patina

shikki/urushi　漆器（しっき）/漆（うるし）lacquerware

DECORATING TECHNIQUES

chinkin　沈金（ちんきん）
　　design created by engraving lines into a lacquered surface, which are filled with lacquer before applying gold dust or leaf

maki-e　蒔絵（まきえ）
　　decoration made of gold or silver dust, nuggets, slivers, and strips; *maki-e* is divided into three types: flat (*hira*), low-relief (*taka*), and burnished (*togidashi*)

maki-e

raden/aogai-zaiku
　螺鈿 （らでん）/青貝細工 （あおがいざいく）
　　mother-of-pearl inlay

tsuishu　堆朱 （ついしゅ）
　　relief carving of designs in lacquer that has been
　　built up by applying many coats

zōgan　象嵌/象眼 （ぞうがん） inlay

raden / aogai-zaiku

PAPER PRODUCTS

Traditional handmade Japanese paper, known as *washi*, is so unlike modern, mass-produced paper that calling it paper is almost an insult. *Washi* is wonderful stuff, both to look at and to touch. Regrettably, individual sheets of *washi* rarely surface at flea markets.

The term "rice paper" is a misnomer. There are various ideas about how the term originated, but the fact is that no paper is made of rice. *Washi* is actually made of one or more of three fibers—paper mulberry (*kōzo*), *mitsumata*, and *ganpi* (there are no English equivalents for the latter two)—though today wood pulp is often added to lower the cost of production.

The entries here cover items traditionally made of Japanese paper. Items now being made in an effort to keep the *washi* craft alive (stationery sets, jewelry boxes, coasters, tissue-box covers, and the like) are excluded.

chōchin　提灯 （ちょうちん） paper lantern

daifuku-chō　大福帳 （だいふくちょう）
　　handwritten ledger or account book; individual pages are often used
　　decoratively (for example, as lampshades)

Echizen-gami　越前紙 （えちぜんがみ）
　　washi document paper; made in Fukui Prefecture

Edo chiyogami　江戸千代紙 （えどちよがみ）
　　highly decorative printed paper of Edo (Tokyo)

fusuma-gami　襖紙 （ふすまがみ）
　　thick *washi* used to paper *fusuma* panels

Edo chiyogami

gasenshi 画仙紙 (がせんし)

calligraphy and ink-painting practice paper; often contains bamboo or rice-straw fiber; inexpensive and highly absorbent, but not durable

hon 本 (ほん) book

ikkanbari 一閑張り (いっかんばり)

object made of lacquered paper or papier-mâché; sometimes refers to a wooden box covered with *washi*

Izumo-shi 出雲紙 (いずもし)

washi produced near the city of Matsue in Shimane Prefecture, made famous by "Living National Treasure" Eishirō Abe

kamiko 紙子 (かみこ)

thick mulberry *washi* historically used as lining for clothing; today used to make garments, *zabuton* (floor cushion) covers, etc.

koyori 紙縒 (こより)

paper "yarn" or twine used to embellish envelopes or wrap gifts for formal occasions; historically used to weave or braid various kinds of containers, which were then lacquered

Kyō chiyogami 京千代紙 (きょうちよがみ)

highly decorative printed paper of Kyoto

Mino-gami 美濃紙 (みのがみ)

washi made in the Mino region of Gifu Prefecture; famous for decorative "watermarks" made with metal stencils

momi-gami もみ紙 (もみがみ)

thick mulberry *washi* that has been kneaded to make it soft and pliable

noshi 熨斗 (のし)

strip of folded paper used to decorate a gift

ōgi/sensu 扇 (おうぎ)/扇子 (せんす)

folding fan

shifu 紙布 (しふ)

clothing woven of paper yarn; often the weft is paper yarn and the warp is cotton

sensu

shikishi 色紙 (しきし)

square "board" made of paper (about 24 cm x 27 cm); used for painting, calligraphy, celebrity autographs, etc.

shōji-gami　障子紙（しょうじがみ）

washi or washi-type paper used for shōji screens; translucent, white paper

tako　凧（たこ）kite

tanzaku　短冊（たんざく）

long sheet of paper used for writing poetry; poem is written vertically

uchiwa　団扇（うちわ）nonfolding fan

wagasa　和傘（わがさ）Japanese umbrella

uchiwa

bangasa　番傘（ばんがさ）

umbrella made of coarse, yellowish oil-paper

janome-gasa　蛇の目傘（じゃのめがさ）

umbrella made of thick dyed paper with a white bull's-eye design, traditionally said to resemble the eye of a snake (janome)

washi　和紙（わし）

traditional handmade Japanese paper; in the early 20th century, there were over a thousand types of washi being produced

wagasa

Yoshino-gami　吉野紙（よしのがみ）

washi made in the Yoshino area of Nara Prefecture; famous for very strong yet extremely thin tissues

PHOTOGRAPHS AND POSTCARDS

Old Japanese photographs are quite rare but much in demand. The best pictures show people, vividly (if somewhat stiffly) captured in a variety of settings: members of a tennis club, dressed in whites and holding their rackets; company employees on an outing to Mt. Fuji; an army officer in uniform; a couple in kimono on their wedding day. This is probably why they are so evocative of their era: they possess a kind of immediacy that most other items sold at flea markets, lacking the visible human element, cannot match.

Postcards and *buromaido* ("bromides") also afford a glimpse of life during the old days, but they are by definition more commercial and generally less compelling.

buromaido　ブロマイド
"bromide," or commercially shot still photograph of an actor or celebrity; these images were avidly and widely collected by fans, so much so that certain specialty outlets sold nothing else

e-hagaki　絵葉書（えはがき）picture postcard

hagaki　葉書（はがき）postcard

kamera　カメラ　camera

kinen shashin　記念写真（きねんしゃしん）
commemorative photograph

shashin　写真（しゃしん）photograph

PRINTS, DRAWINGS, AND SCROLLS

Considering their widespread popularity and entrenched status as Oriental art, prints, drawings, and scrolls are in surprisingly short supply at flea markets. Probably as a result, the quality of those seen tends to fall far short of the quality of those available through art dealers. However, when encountered, they are generally worth checking out, even if the odds don't favor finding one you like.

The images and calligraphy are probably of more interest than the implements used to create them, but on the other hand, items like inkstones and water droppers can be beautiful in their own right and, being both small and individually patterned, make nice collectibles.

abura-e　油絵（あぶらえ）oil painting

bijin-ga　美人画（びじんが）
"picture of beautiful women," an important type of *ukiyo-e*

bunjin-ga/nanga 文人画 （ぶんじんが）/南画 （なんが）
　　literati-style painting popular in the 18th, 19th, and early 20th centuries

butsu-ga 仏画 （ぶつが） Buddhist picture, print, and painting

chizu 地図 （ちず）
　　map; represents a rare and specialized type of woodblock print, nowadays very difficult to obtain, especially if in pristine condition

dōban 銅板 （どうばん） copperplate etching

e 絵 （え） picture, drawing, illustration, painting

ecchingu エッチング etching

emaki/emakimono 絵巻 （えまき）/絵巻物 （えまきもの）
　　picture scroll; unrolled from right to left on a desk or table, not hung

fude 筆 （ふで）
　　traditional Japanese or Chinese writing brush

fusuma-e 襖絵 （ふすまえ）
　　picture painted on *fusuma* panel

gakubuchi 額縁 （がくぶち） picture frame

gi-ga 戯画 （ぎが） comic picture; usually *ukiyo-e*

hai-ga 俳画 （はいが）
　　minimalist ink painting associated with haiku

hanga/mokuhan 版画 （はんが）/木版 （もくはん）
woodblock print

fude

hangi 版木 （はんぎ） carved wooden printing block

hanzaishiki 半彩色 （はんざいしき）
　　picture composed of black lines printed with woodblock and areas of color applied by hand; many Buddhist and Shinto pictures are of this type

hyōgu/hyōsō
　　表具 （ひょうぐ）/表装 （ひょうそう）
　　traditional Japanese scroll mounting

hyōshi 表紙 （ひょうし）
　　jacket or cover of book, magazine, etc.

hanga

jiku/jikubō　軸（じく）/軸棒（じくぼう）
  bottom bar of a hanging scroll

kakejiku/kakemono　掛け軸（かけじく）/掛け物（かけもの）
  hanging scroll

o-kyō　お経（おきょう）Buddhist sutra

Nihon-ga　日本画（にほんが）traditional Japanese-style painting

nishiki-e　錦絵（にしきえ）
  polychrome *ukiyo-e* print (literally, "brocade picture")

sansui-ga　山水画（さんすいが）
  Chinese-style landscape painting, either *sumi-e*
  or colored

sashi-e/irasuto　挿し絵（さしえ）/イラスト
  illustration in book, magazine, newspaper, etc.

sekiban　石版（せきばん）lithograph

sho　書（しょ）calligraphy

shun-ga　春画（しゅんが）
  pornographic print or painting

sansui-ga

suisai　水彩（すいさい）watercolor drawing

suiteki　水滴（すいてき）
  dropper used to pour water on inkstone for mixing ink

sumi　墨（すみ）
  black ink in the form of a stick, block, or disk

sumi-e　墨絵（すみえ）
  traditional Japanese drawing, illustration, or brush painting done in
  black ink

suzuri　硯（すずり）
  stone used to make black ink; the artist pours a
  small amount of water from a dropper (*suiteki*)
  into a depression in the stone, then he dips an ink
  stick (*sumi*) in the water and rubs it against the
  stone; after mixing the ink, he uses the piece of stone
  as an ink well, dipping his brush into it as he works

suzuri

uchiwa-e 団扇絵 （うちわえ）picture drawn on a folding fan

ukiyo-e 浮世絵 （うきよえ）

literally "picture of the floating world"; a vibrant, colorful woodblock print, originally depicting courtesans, kabuki actors, and subjects associated with the pleasure quarters of Edo; *ukiyo-e* landscapes and everyday scenes of village or city life developed in the early 19th century

yakusha-e 役者絵 （やくしゃえ）
ukiyo-e picture of kabuki actor

yatate 矢立て （やたて）
portable case or holder for brush and ink; used when traveling

yō-ga 洋画 （ようが）
Western-style picture, painting

Zen-ga 禅画 （ぜんが）Zen painting

RELIGIOUS AND CEREMONIAL OBJECTS

Religious and ceremonial objects are some of the most distinctive items found at flea markets. Since many of them are made for use in temples, shrines, and festivals, they tend to be of high quality. For the same reason, they tend to carry high price tags and to come into circulation infrequently—especially the larger or heavier items, such as portable shrines and statues. However, with patience and persistence they can be found, and many are one of a kind.

butsudan 仏壇 （ぶつだん）household Buddhist altar

chōkoku 彫刻 （ちょうこく）sculpture

daruma 達磨 （だるま）

daruma

colorfully painted papier-mâché doll representing Bodhidharma; the eyes are not drawn in—its owner is supposed to draw in the doll's right eye and make a wish, then draw in the left eye if the wish comes true

ema   絵馬（えま）

votive picture; usually painted on a wooden tablet

kamidana   神棚（かみだな）

household Shinto shrine

kane   鐘（かね）bell

komainu   狛犬（こまいぬ）

guardian dog statues at Shinto shrines; a pair of them flanks the shrine entrance

mikoshi   神輿（みこし）

portable shrine said to embody a god or divine spirit; hoisted on the shoulders and carried through the streets by participants in festivals

mokugyo   木魚（もくぎょ）

hollow wooden percussion instrument in the shape of a fish; struck by Buddhist priest during chants and ceremonies

rin/kane/kin   鈴（りん/かね/きん）

bell rung by Buddhist priest during chants and ceremonies; known by three different names

saisen-bako   賽銭箱（さいせんばこ）

temple offertory box; worshippers insert coins or bills into slot or opening

sanbō   三方（さんぼう）

stand on which an offering of food or drink to the gods is placed

shishigashira   獅子頭（ししがしら）

carved head of a *shishi*, often translated as "lion" or "lion-dog"; most important prop in the lion dance performed at festivals

shishigashira

shuinchō   朱印帖（しゅいんちょう）

book for collecting commemorative stamps of temples and shrines

taiko   太鼓（たいこ）drum

teppatsu   鉄鉢（てっぱつ）lacquerware Buddhist begging bowl

zō 像（ぞう）statue, sculpture

    butsuzō 仏像（ぶつぞう）statue of Buddha

    chōzō 彫像（ちょうぞう）carved statue

    dōzō 銅像（どうぞう）bronze statue

    mokuzō 木像（もくぞう）wooden statue

    sekizō 石像（せきぞう）stone statue

zushi 厨子（ずし）

    cabinet usually consisting of a Buddha statue housed in a templelike wooden box with doors and sometimes a roof

butsuzō

TEA CEREMONY IMPLEMENTS

The practice of the tea ceremony has resulted in the production of numerous specially designed, found-only-in-Japan items—from teapots and tea bowls to ladles, whisks, scoops, and trivets. Like the tea ceremony itself, all these items possess what the Japanese call *wabi sabi*, a calm atmosphere; a beauty born of simplicity; and a quiet, almost spiritual, power.

While many of these items do not often surface at flea markets, when they do, their refined design and understated elegance makes them worth pursuing.

chagama/kama 茶釜/釜（ちゃがま/かま）
    cast-iron vessel used to heat water

chasen 茶筅（ちゃせん）tea whisk

chashaku 茶杓（ちゃしゃく）
    tea scoop for powdered tea; usually made of bamboo

chawan/matcha-jawan 茶碗（ちゃわん）/
    抹茶茶碗（まっちゃぢゃわん）
    tea bowl; the first term sometimes refers to a rice bowl or a bowl about the size of a rice bowl

chasen

dora 銅鑼（どら）gong

furo 風炉 （ふろ）
  brazier/hearth for heating water

furosaki byōbu 風炉先屏風 （ふろさきびょうぶ）
  screen placed behind *furo*

futa oki 蓋置き （ふたおき） rest for lid of water container

gotoku 五徳 （ごとく） trivet for holding *chagama*

haiki 灰器 （はいき） ash dish

haisaji 灰匙 （はいさじ） ash scoop

hane 羽 （はね） feather duster

hibashi 火箸 （ひばし）
  metal chopsticks for handling coals

hishaku 柄杓 （ひしゃく）
  water ladle; made of bamboo

hishaku

ita/shiki-ita 板 （いた）/敷板 （しきいた） tile plaque for *furo*

kan 鐶 （かん） kettle rings (handles)

kensui 建水 （けんすい） waste-water container

mizusashi 水指し （みずさし） water container

mizutsugi 水次ぎ （みずつぎ） water pitcher

natsume/chaki/cha-ire なつめ/茶器 （ちゃき）/茶入 （ちゃいれ）
  tea container (*natsume* and *chaki* are for "thin tea," *cha-ire* is for
  "thick tea")

robuchi 炉縁 （ろぶち） frame around hearth

sumitori 炭斗 （すみとり） charcoal basket

tana 棚 （たな） utensil stand/shelves

futa oki

natsume

TEXTILES

Japan is a textile country; at one time, practically every rural house had an active loom. As a result, the range of traditional textiles is immense, ranging from indigo-dyed cottons to silk brocades and gossamers. Virtually every flea market today has vendors selling textiles, from wrapping cloths and hand towels to comforter covers and shop curtains.

It is helpful in appreciating the artistry of Japanese textiles to understand something of how they are made. To that end, some of the entries in this section explain the basics of traditional methods of textile production.

Traditional Japanese textiles fall into three groups: those dyed after being woven (referred to as dyed), those dyed before being woven (referred to as woven) and those that are stitched or embroidered (these can be either dyed or woven). These groups are covered in the first three sections below.

The fourth section covers nonclothing textile items. The fifth section gives the Japanese names of the natural fibers from which virtually all traditional Japanese textiles are made.

DYEING AND DYED TEXTILES

aizome　藍染め（あいぞめ）

aizome

indigo, a blue dye most often used to dye folk textiles made of cotton or hemp

gojiru　豆汁（ごじる）

soy milk, applied before dyeing to aid dye penetration

itajime　板締め（いたじめ）

a dyeing technique in which folded cloth is clamped between boards, which may have cut-out designs

kanoko　鹿の子（かのこ）

tiny dots used to fill in areas of fabric; creates a mottled effect

katagami　型紙（かたがみ）

paper stencil used in *katazome*; traditionally constructed of two or three layers of durable *washi* coated with persimmon tannin

Ise katagami　伊勢型紙（いせかたがみ）

textile-dyeing paper stencil made in the Ise area of Mie Prefecture

katazome 型染め（かたぞめ）

paste-resist dyeing technique in which designs are applied through stencils

komon 小紋（こもん）

fabric completely covered with minute stenciled pattern

nori 糊（のり）

paste used as resist in dyeing process; made from a mixture of powdered glutinous rice and rice bran

katazome

sarasa 更紗（さらさ）

"printed" Indian cotton or any fabric resembling it; often used as a generic term for any exotic or tropical-looking fabric

shibori 絞り（しぼり）

a family of dyeing techniques, often referred to as "Japanese tie-dye," in which the cloth is tied, folded, clamped, or held back during dyeing, to keep some areas from taking color

shinshi 伸子（しんし）

tenter; used to stretch a bolt of cloth to facilitate the drawing of a design, dyeing, and drying

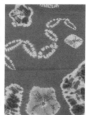

shibori

tsutsugaki 筒描き（つつがき）

paste-resist dyeing technique in which designs are drawn freehand with a paste applicator (like a pastry cone); *tsutsugaki* differs from *tegaki yūzen* in that indigo is the background color and the fabric is usually cotton

yūzen 友禅（ゆうぜん）

dyeing technique that combines fine lines of paste-resist with delicate hand painting

kata yūzen 型友禅（かたゆうぜん）

yūzen incorporating stencil designs; the same process is used as for *tegaki yūzen*, except that designs are created by applying dye-infused paste through paper stencils; when the paste is washed off, the dyes remain

tegaki yūzen 手描き友禅（てがきゆうぜん）

yūzen incorporating freehand designs: a design is first drawn on the fabric with a temporary color. The lines of the design are covered with rice-paste resist using an applicator (like a pastry cone). Soy milk is applied to the fabric to aid dye penetration. Dye is brushed into each motif or design area and the fabric is steamed to set the dyes. Then the resist paste is washed away. The base color is applied last, after covering the area occupied by the completed design with resist paste.

WEAVING AND WOVEN TEXTILES

aya ori 綾織 (あやおり)

twill, or fabric containing diagonal patterns in the weave itself; these patterns, which are revealed by reflected light, are created by weaving weft threads over or under two or more warp threads

bashōfu 芭蕉布 (ばしょうふ)

Okinawan cloth woven from plantain (banana) fiber

chijimi 縮み (ちぢみ)

crepe cloth; usually made of silk or cotton

chirimen 縮緬 (ちりめん)

silk crepe made by twisting alternating weft threads in opposite directions

Hakata ori 博多織 (はかたおり)

stiff, ribbed, plain weave cloth only used to make *obi*; it is well suited to this purpose because it keeps the bow from slipping or coming untied; usually made of silk

hira ori 平織り (ひらおり)

flat or plain weave; weft threads go over and under alternating threads of the warp

kara ori 唐織 (からおり)

float-weave brocade, a type of satin with "floating" silk threads which lay on top of the fabric like embroidery; generally seen only in Noh and kabuki costumes, *uchikake*, and very expensive *obi*

karami ori からみ織 (からみおり)

gauzelike silk fabric with loose, open mesh

kasuri　絣（かすり）

> ikat; cloth woven from threads dyed with a pattern before being woven, resulting in a pattern with "blurry" edges

nishiki　錦（にしき）brocade; usually silk

orimono　織物（おりもの）

> woven item, cloth, fabric, material

ro　絽（ろ）silk gauze weave

kasuri

saki ori　裂き織（さきおり）rag weave (cloth woven from rags)

sha　紗（しゃ）silk leno weave

tsumugi　紬（つむぎ）

> pongee; fabric woven from hand-spun yarn made from the silk floss of imperfect or damaged cocoons; the fabric has a rough finish

tsuzure ori　綴れ織（つづれおり）

> fine silk tapestry weave

TEXTILES WITH NEEDLEWORK OR APPLIED DECORATION

kogin　小巾（こぎん）

> highly decorative variation of *sashiko* made in the northern region of Honshū

nuihaku　縫い箔（ぬいはく）

> combination of embroidery and imprinted gold or silver leaf

kogin

Saga nishiki　佐賀錦（さがにしき）

> brocade of silk combining gold or silver warp and colored weft; often used for kimono accessories

sashiko　刺し子（さしこ）

> quilting with heavy thread and decorative stitchwork used to strengthen and give added warmth to the indigo-dyed work clothes of farmers and fishermen

shishū　刺繍（ししゅう）embroidery

shishū

furoshiki　風呂敷 （ふろしき）
　　square cloth for wrapping and carrying things

futon no kawa / futongawa
　　蒲団のかわ （ふとんのかわ）/ 布団がわ （ふとんがわ）
　　futon cover

furoshiki

mōfu　毛布 （もうふ） blanket

noren　暖簾 （のれん）
　　split curtain hung in a doorway

noren

uma no haragake
　　馬の腹掛け （うまのはらがけ）
　　horse trapping (cloth draped over a horse
　　on ceremonial occasions)

zabuton　座蒲団 （ざぶとん）
　　thick, square floor cushion

zabuton

ama　亜麻 （あま） flax/linen

asa　麻 （あさ）
　　hemp; catch-all term used by dealers for cloth woven of any rough fiber

jōfu / choma　上布 （じょうふ）/ 苧麻 （ちょま） ramie

kinu / shiruku　絹 （きぬ）/ シルク　silk

momen　木綿 （もめん） cotton

tafu　太布 （たふ）
　　generic term for cloth woven of rough fibers and bast fibers such as
　　hemp or *kōzo* and *shina* tree bark

ūru　ウール　wool

TRADITIONAL GARMENTS

Beautiful old kimono, *obi* (kimono sashes), and related garments, no longer worn every day, are to be found at every flea market. Sometimes they are whole, sometimes in pieces. Either way, the shopper has attractive options, as the idea is not to wear the item (although a *yukata* used as a bathrobe is possible) but to display it (a kimono or *uchikake* makes a wall hanging, an *obi* can be converted into a table runner) or to create something new (pieces of material can be turned into place mats, coasters, pillow covers). For anyone with more advanced sewing ability, new clothes can be fashioned from old (a blouse can be made from silk, a shirt or light jacket from indigo-dyed cotton), and for quilters or collage makers, scraps of fabric, available in quantity and very affordable, present a wealth of creative opportunities.

This section covers kimono, accessories including the *obi*, and garments closely related to or used in conjunction with the kimono, like the *haori* and *uchikake*.

geta 下駄 (げた) wooden clogs

hachimaki 鉢巻 (はちまき)
tenugui twisted and tied around a man's head as a sweatband

geta

hakama 袴 (はかま)
pleated culottes worn over kimono and paired with *haori* for male formal wear

haori 羽織 (はおり)
men's or women's jacket, waist-length or slightly longer

haori

happi/hanten 法被/半纏 (はっぴ/はんてん)
waist-length jacket made of lightweight cotton worn by participants in festivals and workers in certain occupations

hikeshi-banten 火消し半纏 (ひけしばんてん)
thick cotton fireman's coat, quilted and often colorfully decorated

juban 襦袢 (じゅばん)
lightweight robe, usually made of silk, worn under kimono; only the edge of the robe is visible along the collar

han-juban 半襦袢 (はんじゅばん)
    short *juban*

naga-juban 長襦袢 (ながじゅばん)
    long *juban*

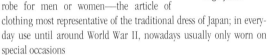

naga-juban

kanzashi 簪 (かんざし) ornamental hairpin

kimono 着物 (きもの)
    full-length, lined or unlined, silk or cotton
    robe for men or women—the article of
    clothing most representative of the traditional dress of Japan; in every-
    day use until around World War II, nowadays usually only worn on
    special occasions

> **furisode** 振袖 (ふりそで)
>   long-sleeved kimono, characterized by bright
>   colors and large motifs, traditionally worn
>   by young (unmarried) women
>
> **tomesode** 留袖 (とめそで)
>   formal black or colored kimono bearing
>   either three or five small family crests; worn
>   at occasions such as weddings and funerals

furisode

kōgai 笄 (こうがい)
    stick-like accessory traditionally used as an
    ornamental hairpin

koshi himo 腰紐 (こしひも)
    sash used to hold up the excess length of the
    kimono; tucked at the waist just below the *obi*

tomesode

kushi 櫛 (くし)
    traditional comb; made of boxwood or tortoiseshell

maekake 前掛け (まえかけ) apron

monpe もんぺ
    baggy cotton pantaloon-style work pants, gath-
    ered at the ankles; usually worn by women and
    decorated with *kasuri* designs

montsuki 紋付き (もんつき)
    formal kimono decorated with *mon* (family
    crest)

kushi

obi 帯 （おび）

> sash worn with kimono, wrapped around the waist to keep it closed, tied in a knot or a bow

fukuro obi 袋帯 （ふくろおび）

> double-fold formal *obi*; the inner surface is plain and the outer more than sixty percent covered with design

hanhaba obi 半幅帯 （はんはばおび）

> half-width *obi* worn with casual kimono or *yukata*

maru obi 丸帯 （まるおび）

> double-width formal *obi* made of heavy fabric; inner and outer surfaces completely covered with design

Nagoya obi 名古屋帯 （なごやおび）

> narrow, lightweight *obi* folded in half and sewn closed along half its length

maru obi

obiage 帯揚げ （おびあげ）

> silk scarflike piece of cloth tucked into the top of the *obi*

obidome 帯止め （おびどめ）

clasp used to fasten the *obijime*

obijime 帯締め （おびじめ）

> narrow silk cord that helps hold together the bow tied at the back of the *obi*

pokkuri ぽっくり

> traditional footwear worn by girl until marriage; a kind of *geta*

tabi 足袋 （たび） split-toed, ankle-high socks

tenugui 手拭い （てぬぐい）

> long cotton hand towel, often with stenciled designs

uchikake 打ち掛け （うちかけ）

> elaborately embroidered silk coat worn by the bride over a plain white kimono at a wedding ceremony

yogi 夜着 （よぎ）

> thick, padded winter bed cover in the shape of a kimono

yukata 浴衣 (ゆかた)

  lightweight cotton kimono; worn in summer, especially at festivals, and used year-round as a sort of bathrobe

zōri 草履 (ぞうり) thong sandals worn with kimono

MISCELLANEOUS

This is a catch-all category containing items, including a few weapons, that do not fall into the other categories.

Hakone zaiku 箱根細工 (はこねざいく)

  decorative carpentry technique utilizing woods of different colors, which are arranged in intricate patterns

hōseki 宝石 (ほうせき) jewels, jewelry

hyōtan 瓢箪 (ひょうたん)

  gourd; Japanese gourds usually have the double-bulb shape, with top smaller than bottom

Hakone zaiku

inrō 印籠 (いんろう)

  pill box or small medicine case; hung from sash or belt of samurai or merchant

kabuto 兜 (かぶと) helmet

katana 刀 (かたな) sword

katana-kake 刀掛け (かたなかけ)

  sword rest, a sort of rack on which a sheathed sword is placed horizontally

inrō

kiriko 切子 (きりこ) cut glass

kiseru 煙管 (きせる) thin metal pipe for smoking tobacco

kiseru

maneki-neko   招き猫（まねきねこ）
"inviting cat" displayed in the front of a shop or restaurant; with its left or right paw raised in a gesture of beckoning, It is said to bring more customers

megane   目鏡（めがね）eyeglasses; spectacles

men   面（めん）/お面（おめん）mask

menō   瑪瑙（めのう）agate

naginata   長刀/薙刀（なぎなた）halberd

netsuke   根付（ねつけ）
carving to hold *inrō* or tobacco pouch in place

nōmen   能面（のうめん）Noh mask

nōmen

o-haguro   お歯黒（おはぐろ）
lacquerware vessel used to hold the materials for blackening the teeth, a custom of married women during the Edo period

rashingi   羅針儀（らしんぎ）compass (for steering or navigation)

soroban   算盤（そろばん）abacus

soroban

tabakoire   煙草入れ（たばこいれ）
tobacco pouch made from leather or cloth

ya   矢（や）arrow

yari   槍/鎗（やり）spear

yoroi   鎧（よろい）armor

yumi   弓（ゆみ）bow

V. FLEA-MARKET JAPANESE

Having the language skills needed to find and bargain for what you want makes all the difference to flea-market shopping. Most vendors know little or no English, let alone other languages, so learning the Japanese needed to talk to them is crucial.

This section is designed to help you do just that. It contains a "Survival Kit" of over 150 words, phrases and model sentences carefully chosen to help you cope with the most frequently encountered shopping situations—browsing, asking about things to buy, bargaining, and so on.

A minimum language ability level of lower-intermediate is needed to make the most of the linguistic tools provided. Beginners and nonspeakers of Japanese can just point to the words on the page.

NOTE: The English and Japanese versions do not always correspond in literal, word-for-word fashion, but the translation is natural and correct in context. The language is neutral-polite (*teineigo*)—with -*masu* verb endings and the use of *desu* at the end of sentences—so it neither humbles the shopper nor exalts the vendor. Depending on the situation, you may wish to change the level of politeness to humble-polite (*kensongo*) or respectful-polite (*sonkeigo*).

In Japanese, when the subject of a sentence is understood from the context of the situation, it is often left unstated. Sample sentences for which this rule applies may show the subject of the sentence, usually indicated by the particle *wa*, in parentheses.

Uttering the appropriate greetings and using proper courtesy language is vital to communicating effectively with Japanese. Formalities that may be dispensed with in the West should, in Japan, be used during every interaction. Mastering a few simple phrases will help you to ease some of the apprehension many Japanese feel when meeting foreigners and may lead to a better explanation of something you want to buy—or to a lower price.

good morning
ohayō gozaimasu
おはようございます

hello
konnichi wa
今日は

please (when offering something)
dōzo
どうぞ

please (when asking for something to be done)
o-negai shimasu
お願いします

thank you (very much)
(*dōmo*) *arigatō* (*gozaimasu*)
（どうも）ありがとう（ございます）

excuse me/I'm sorry
sumimasen (or *suimasen*)
gomen-nasai
すみません（すいません）
ごめんなさい

---

goodbye
sayōnara (or *sayonara*)
さようなら（さよなら）

---

see you again
de wa mata
ではまた

(I hope to) see you soon.
Mata chikai uchi ni o-ai shimashō.
また近いうちにお会いしましょう。

BROWSING

Although choosing what to buy can be difficult, browsing is easy if you know the phrases in this section. But there are a few things to bear in mind. First, it can be hard to tell whether or not an object is for sale, since a table, chest, or screen used to display merchandise may be an antique itself. If in doubt, ask, using the sentence for that purpose provided below. Second, saying "I'd like to buy _____" signals that you are ready to start bargaining, so be prepared to start negotiating a price immediately. Third, to indicate politely that you are not interested in an item, saying "*kangaete okimasu*" ("I'll think it over") should suffice. When a stronger way of saying "no" is needed, as when a vendor gives you the hard sell, use "_____ *wa irimasen*" ("I don't want/need _____").

I'm looking for _____. (Do you have any _____?)

_____ *o sagashite imasu ga ...*

_____ を探していますが ...

Do you have _____?

_____ *wa arimasu ka?*

_____ はありますか?

Please show me _____ .

_____ *o misete kudasai.*

_____ を見せて下さい。

May I look at _____?

_____ *o mite mo ii desu ka?*

_____ を見てもいいですか?

May I touch _____?

_____ *o sawatte mo ii desu ka?*

_____ を触ってもいいですか?

Is _____ for sale?

_____ *wa urimono desu ka?*

_____ は売り物ですか?

I'd like to buy _____.

_____ *o kaitai no desu ga ...*

_____ を買いたいのですが ...

How much are you asking for _____?

(_____ wa) ikura desu ka?

(_____ は) いくらですか？

I'll think it over.

Kangaete okimasu.

考えておきます。

I don't want/need _____ .

(_____ wa) irimasen.

(_____ は) いりません。

Sample Word Substitutions	
this/that	*kore/sore/are*
this/that (item)	*kono/sono/ano* (item)
this chest	*kono tansu*

ASKING ABOUT THINGS TO BUY

The questions below, particularly those that are open-ended, allow you to gather a wealth of information about the object you are interested in. The quantity and quality of information you get depends in part on the vendor's personality (and other factors beyond your control). Be prepared for answers ranging from the monosyllabic to the long-winded, and be ready to do some polite probing, or interrupting, depending on your partner's conversational style.

For help figuring out how old something is, refer to the table listing historical eras, or consult the chart giving the year of the Western calendar for each year of the Japanese calendar from the beginning of the Meiji era to the present. If you are unsure about counters, refer to the table showing the counters used most often.

What is _____?

(_____ wa) nan desu ka?

(_____ は) 何ですか?

Please tell me about _____ .

_____ ni tsuite oshiete kudasai.

_____ について教えて下さい。

What was _____ originally used for?

(_____ wa) moto moto nan ni tsukatte imashita ka?

(_____ は) もともと何に使っていましたか?

How (many years) old is _____?

(_____ wa) doregurai furui desu ka?

(_____ は) どれぐらい古いですか?

What historical period does _____ date from?

(_____ wa) jidai wa itsu desu ka?

(_____ は) 時代はいつですか?

What is the geographic origin of _____?

(_____ wa) doko no mono desu ka?

(_____ は) どこのものですか?

What material is _____ made of?

(_____ wa) nan de dekite imasu ka?

(_____ は) 何でできていますか?

Does _____ have any damage or defects?

(_____ wa) kizu ga arimasu ka?

(_____ は) 傷がありますか?

Does _____ work (properly)?

(_____ wa) (chanto) ugokimasu ka?

(_____ は) (ちゃんと) 動きますか?

(Besides its original purpose) what could _____ be used for?

(_____ wa) nan ni tsukaeba ii desu ka?

(_____ は) 何に使えばいいですか?

Is _____ being sold as part of a set or individually?

(_____ wa) setto desu ka? Soretomo tanpin desu ka?

(_____ は) セットですか? それとも単品ですか?

Is it okay to buy only _____ of these, not the whole set?

_____ dake demo ii desu ka?

_____ だけでもいいですか?

Sample Word Substitutions	
this/that	*kore/sore/are*
this/that (thing to buy)	*kono/sono/ano* (thing to buy)
(counter)	*hitotsu, san-mai, go-ko* (see Counters)

Historical Eras

In discussing the age of antiques, you should know the dates of the five most recent Japanese historical eras, listed in the table below. (Earlier eras are excluded because pre–Edo-period antiques almost never appear at flea markets.) Knowing an antique's age helps you assess its value.

A vendor may not know an antique's exact age—it is often difficult to judge an antique's age with any precision. In such cases, the vendor may simply say "It's from the _____ era," or hazard a guess, along the lines of, "Well, it's from about the beginning of Meiji. At least, I think so."

QUESTION (SHOPPER):

What historical period does _____ date from?

(_____ wa) jidai wa itsu desu ka?

(_____ は) 時代はいつですか？

ANSWER (VENDOR):

It dates from (about) the _____ of) the _____ period.

_____ jidai (no _____) (gurai) desu.

_____ 時代 (の _____) (ぐらい) です。

HISTORICAL ERAS (*JIDAI*)			hajime	始め	beginning
			zenhan	前半	first half
Edo	江戸	1603–1868	nakaba	半ば	middle
Meiji	明治	1868–1912	kōhan	後半	last half
Taishō	大正	1912–26	owari	終わり	end
Shōwa	昭和	1926–89	shoki	初期	early
Heisei	平成	1989–present	chūki	中期	middle
			kōki	後期	late

The Japanese Calendar

This chart equates years on the Japanese calendar with years on the Western calendar, from the beginning of the Meiji era to the present.

While vendors usually won't be able to tell you the exact age of an antique, some objects, such as commemorative photographs, prints, and the occasional ceramic piece, are signed and dated.

Meiji (明治)

明治1年	1868	2	1869	3	1870	4	1871	5	1872
6	1873	7	1874	8	1875	9	1876	10	1877
11	1878	12	1879	13	1880	14	1881	15	1882
16	1883	17	1884	18	1885	19	1886	20	1887
21	1888	22	1889	23	1890	24	1891	25	1892
26	1893	27	1894	28	1895	29	1896	30	1897
31	1898	32	1899	33	1900	34	1901	35	1902
36	1903	37	1904	38	1905	39	1906	40	1907
41	1908	42	1909	43	1910	44	1911	45	1912

Taishō (大正)

大正1年	1912	2	1913	3	1914	4	1915	5	1916
6	1917	7	1918	8	1919	9	1920	10	1921
11	1922	12	1923	13	1924	14	1925	15	1926

Shōwa (昭和)

昭和1年	1926	2	1927	3	1928	4	1929	5	1930
6	1931	7	1932	8	1933	9	1934	10	1935
11	1936	12	1937	13	1938	14	1939	15	1940
16	1941	17	1942	18	1943	19	1944	20	1945
21	1946	22	1947	23	1948	24	1949	25	1950
26	1951	27	1952	28	1953	29	1954	30	1955
31	1956	32	1957	33	1958	34	1959	35	1960
36	1961	37	1962	38	1963	39	1964	40	1965
41	1966	42	1967	43	1968	44	1969	45	1970
46	1971	47	1972	48	1973	49	1974	50	1975
51	1976	52	1977	53	1978	54	1979	55	1980
56	1981	57	1982	58	1983	59	1984	60	1985
61	1986	62	1987	63	1988	64	1989		

Heisei (平成)

平成1年	1989	2	1990	3	1991	4	1992	5	1993
6	1994	7	1995	8	1996	9	1997	10	1998
11	1999	12	2000	13	2001	14	2002	15	2003
16	2004	17	2005	18	2006	19	2007	20	2008
21	2009	22	2010							

Counters

Counters are special words used, as the name suggests, to count objects—one chest of drawers, two hanging scrolls, three plates, and so on. A difficulty in Japanese is that different types of objects require different counters, depending on their shape and other properties; consequently, there are scores of counters in use. This makes· it a challenge to learn which goes with which.

Fortunately, the difficulty can be avoided by using the so-called generic counter, appropriate for any type of object. This series, shown below, ends in -*tsu*. Also shown below—mainly for reference—are a few of the most common nongeneric counters. The Usage Guide pairs the counters with various types of objects and gives examples of items at flea markets that qualify as each type.

COUNTER		-*tsu*	-*dai*	-*hon*	-*ko*	-*kumi*	-*mai*
	1	*hito-tsu*	*ichi-dai*	*ip-pon*	*ik-ko*	*hito-kumi*	*ichi-mai*
	2	*futa-tsu*	*ni-dai*	*ni-hon*	*ni-ko*	*futa-kumi*	*ni-mai*
NUMBER OF OBJECTS	3	*mit-tsu*	*san-dai*	*san-bon*	*san-ko*	*san-kumi*	*san-mai*
	4	*yo-tsu*	*yon-dai*	*yon-hon*	*yon-ko*	*yon-kumi*	*yon-mai*
	5	*itsu-tsu*	*go-dai*	*go-hon*	*go-ko*	*go-kumi*	*go-mai*
	6	*mut-tsu*	*roku-dai*	*rop-pon*	*rok-ko*	*rok-kumi*	*roku-mai*
	7	*nana-tsu*	*nana-dai*	*nana-hon*	*nana-ko*	*nana-kumi*	*nana-mai*
	8	*yat-tsu*	*hachi-dai*	*hap-pon*	*hak-ko*	*hachi-kumi*	*hachi-mai*
	9	*kokono-tsu*	*kyū-dai*	*kyū-hon*	*kyū-ko*	*kyū-kumi*	*kyū-mai*
	10	*tō*	*jū-dai*	*jup-pon*	*juk-ko*	*jū-kumi*	*jū-mai*
HOW MANY?		*iku-tsu?*	*nan-dai?*	*nan-bon?*	*nan-ko?*	*nan-kumi?*	*nan-mai?*

Usage Guide

COUNTER	TYPE OF OBJECT	EXAMPLE MERCHANDISE
-*tsu*	any inanimate object	any merchandise
-*dai*	vehicle, machine, piece of furniture	cart, spinning wheel, dresser
-*hon*	long, cylindrical object	scroll, shovel, set of chopsticks
-*ko*	round or irregularly shaped object	*go* stone, chess piece
-*kumi*	set or group of objects	set of saké cups, set of dolls
-*mai*	thin, flat object	plate, print, poster, piece of fabric

BARGAINING

Bargaining is an inescapable part of flea-market shopping. Your ability to bargain is largely a function of your ability to use the language below—skillfully *and politely*. To this end, it is not a bad idea to soften the language, for example, by changing *"kudasai"* to *"kudasaimasen ka."* If you have trouble saying or understanding amounts of money, refer to the table of numbers.

How much are you asking for _____?
(_____ wa) ikura desu ka?
(_____ は) いくらですか？

Please lower your price.
Nedan o sagete kudasai.
値段を下げて下さい。
Yasuku shite kudasai.
安くしてく下さい。

Please offer a discount.
Benkyō shite kudasai.
勉強して下さい。
Disukaunto shite kudasai.
ディスカウントして下さい。

Your price is (still) a bit high.
(Mada) chotto takai desu.
(まだ) ちょっと高いです。
(Mada) chotto kitsui desu.
(まだ) ちょっときついです。

Your offer of _____ yen is (still) unacceptable.

_____ *yen de wa (mada) dame desu.*

_____ 円では（まだ）だめです。

My (counter)offer is _____ yen.

_____ *yen wa dō desu ka?*

_____ 円はどうですか？

_____ yen is my final offer.

_____ *yen ga rasuto puraisu desu.*

_____ 円がラストプライスです。

Please throw _____ in for free.

_____ *o o-make shite kudasai.*

_____ をおまけして下さい。

I agree to your price of _____ yen.

_____ *yen de daijōbu desu.*

_____ 円で大丈夫です。

_____ *yen de OK desu.*

_____ 円でOKです。

Numbers

Use the chart below to review numbers or convert them into prices. Since flea-market prices are almost always rounded to the nearest 100 or 500 yen, the "milestone" numbers starting with 100 will prove more useful than the numbers from 1 to 99.

As in English, "long" numbers are composed of strings, or sequences, of "short" ones. Thus, 10,485 is "*ichi-man, yon-hyaku, hachi-jū-go.*" To turn a number into a price, simply add "*en*" (yen): 5,500 (*go-sen-go-hyaku*) becomes 5,500 *en* (*go-sen-go-hyaku en*), and so on. Prices are written with the symbol for yen either in front (as in ¥5,500) or behind (as in 5,500円), but in speech the "*en*" always follows the number.

0	*zero*	零	19	*jū-ku*	十九	38	*san-jū-hachi*	三十八
1	*ichi*	一	20	*ni-jū*	二十	39	*san-jū-ku*	三十九
2	*ni*	二	21	*ni-jū-ichi*	二十一	40	*yon-jū*	四十
3	*san*	三	22	*ni-jū-ni*	二十二	41	*yon-jū-ichi*	四十一
4	*yon* (*shi*)	四	23	*ni-jū-san*	二十三	42	*yon-jū-ni*	四十二
5	*go*	五	24	*ni-jū-yon*	二十四	43	*yon-jū-san*	四十三
6	*roku*	六	25	*ni-jū-go*	二十五	44	*yon-jū-yon*	四十四
7	*nana* (*shichi*)	七	26	*ni-jū-roku*	二十六	45	*yon-jū-go*	四十五
8	*hachi*	八	27	*ni-jū-nana*	二十七	46	*yon-jū-roku*	四十六
9	*kyū* (*ku*)	九	28	*ni-jū-hachi*	二十八	47	*yon-jū-nana*	四十七
10	*jū*	十	29	*ni-jū-ku*	二十九	48	*yon-jū-hachi*	四十八
11	*jū-ichi*	十一	30	*san-jū*	三十	49	*yon-jū-ku*	四十九
12	*jū-ni*	十二	31	*san-jū-ichi*	三十一	50	*go-jū*	五十
13	*jū-san*	十三	32	*san-jū-ni*	三十二	51	*go-jū-ichi*	五十一
14	*jū-yon*	十四	33	*san-jū-san*	三十三	52	*go-jū-ni*	五十二
15	*jū-go*	十五	34	*san-jū-yon*	三十四	53	*go-jū-san*	五十三
16	*jū-roku*	十六	35	*san-jū-go*	三十五	54	*go-jū-yon*	五十四
17	*jū-nana*	十七	36	*san-jū-roku*	三十六	55	*go-jū-go*	五十五
18	*jū-hachi*	十八	37	*san-jū-nana*	三十七	56	*go-jū-roku*	五十六

57 *go-jū-nana*	五十七	72 *nana-jū-ni*	七十二	87 *hachi-jū-nana*	八十七		
58 *go-jū-hachi*	五十八	73 *nana-jū-san*	七十三	88 *hachi-jū-hachi*	八十八		
59 *go-jū-ku*	五十九	74 *nana-jū-yon*	七十四	89 *hachi-jū-ku*	八十九		
60 *roku-jū*	六十	75 *nana-jū-go*	七十五	90 *kyū-jū*	九十		
61 *roku-jū-ichi*	六十一	76 *nana-jū-roku*	七十六	91 *kyū-jū-ichi*	九十一		
62 *roku-jū-ni*	六十二	77 *nana-jū-nana*	七十七	92 *kyū-jū-ni*	九十二		
63 *roku-jū-san*	六十三	78 *nana-jū-hachi*	七十八	93 *kyū-jū-san*	九十三		
64 *roku-jū-yon*	六十四	79 *nana-jū-ku*	七十九	94 *kyū-jū-yon*	九十四		
65 *roku-jū-go*	六十五	80 *hachi-jū*	八十	95 *kyū-jū-go*	九十五		
66 *roku-jū-roku*	六十六	81 *hachi-jū-ichi*	八十一	96 *kyū-jū-roku*	九十六		
67 *roku-jū-nana*	六十七	82 *hachi-jū-ni*	八十二	97 *kyū-jū-nana*	九十七		
68 *roku-jū-hachi*	六十八	83 *hachi-jū-san*	八十三	98 *kyū-jū-hachi*	九十八		
69 *roku-jū-ku*	六十九	84 *hachi-jū-yon*	八十四	99 *kyū-jū-kyū*	九十九		
70 *nana-jū*	七十	85 *hachi-jū-go*	八十五				
71 *nana-jū-ichi*	七十一	86 *hachi-jū-roku*	八十六				

---

100 *hyaku*	百	400 *yon-hyaku*	四百	700 *nana-hyaku*	七百
200 *ni-hyaku*	二百	500 *go-hyaku*	五百	800 *hap-pyaku*	八百
300 *san-byaku*	三百	600 *rop-pyaku*	六百	900 *kyū-hyaku*	九百

1,000 *sen (is-sen)*	千	4,000 *yon-sen*	四千	7,000 *nana-sen*	七千
2,000 *ni-sen*	二千	5,000 *go-sen*	五千	8,000 *has-sen*	八千
3,000 *san-zen*	三千	6,000 *roku-sen*	六千	9,000 *kyū-sen*	九千

10,000 *ichi-man*	一万	40,000 *yon-man*	四万	70,000 *nana-man*	七万
20,000 *ni-man*	二万	50,000 *go-man*	五万	80,000 *hachi-man*	八万
30,000 *san-man*	三万	60,000 *roku-man*	六万	90,000 *kyū-man*	九万

100,000 *jū-man*	十万	400,000 *yon-jū-man*	四十万
200,000 *ni-jū-man*	二十万	500,000 *go-jū-man*	五十万
300,000 *san-jū-man*	十万	1,000,000 *hyaku-man*	百万

Useful Words

The following list of words should be helpful even if you are only able to use it passively, as a means to understand what you hear.

DESCRIBING THINGS TO BUY

Consult this list when describing something to buy. Or, when bargaining, use it to point out damage or a defect (see the words under Condition).

■ SIZE/HEIGHT/WIDTH

size	ōkisa	大きさ
	saizu	サイズ
width	hirosa	広さ
	haba	幅
height	takasa	高さ
big	ōkii	大きい
	ōki na	大きな
	dekkai	でっかい
small	chīsai (chicchai)	小さい (小っちゃい)
	chīsa na	小さな
wide	hiroi	広い
narrow	semai	狭い
tall, high	takai	高い
short, low	hikui	低い

■ COLORS

color	iro	色	green	midori	緑
black	kuro	黒	red	aka	赤
brown	chairo	茶色	pink	pinku	ピンク
beige	bēju	ベージュ	yellow	kiiro	黄色
blue	ao	青	white	shiro	白
	burū	ブルー			

pattern	*gara/monyō*	柄/紋様
	patān	パターン
design	*dezain*	デザイン
motif	*mochīfu*	モチーフ
shape/form	*katachi*	形
style	*sutairu*	スタイル
flat	*taira na/hiratai*	平らな/ひらたい
round	*marui*	丸い
pointed	*togatta*	尖った
sharp	*surudoi*	鋭い

buna	ぶな	beech
hinoki	檜 (ひのき)	Japanese cypress
hō	朴 (ほう)	magnolia
keyaki	欅 (けやき)	paulownia
kiri	桐 (きり)	zelkova
kokutan	黒檀 (こくたん)	ebony
kuri	栗 (くり)	chestnut
matsu	松 (まつ)	pine
nara/kashi	楢/樫 (なら/かし)	oak varieties
sakura	桜 (さくら)	cherry tree
shitan	紫檀 (したん)	red sandalwood
sugi	杉 (すぎ)	cedar (cryptomeria)
yanagi	柳 (やなぎ)	willow

bekkō	鼈甲 (べっこう)	tortoiseshell; traditionally used to make combs, hairpins, and other accessories
bīdoro/garasu	ビードロ/ガラス	glass
dō	銅 (どう)	copper

gin	銀 (ぎん)	silver
hakkin	白金 (はっきん)	platinum
hisui	翡翠 (ひすい)	jade
kin	金 (きん)	gold
sango	珊瑚 (さんご)	coral
seidō	青銅 (せいどう)	bronze
shakudō	赤銅 (しゃくどう)	alloy of copper and gold with a bronze-purple color; used for ornate figures and objects
shinju	真珠 (しんじゅ)	pearl
shippō	七宝 (しっぽう)	cloisonné
suishō	水晶 (すいしょう)	crystal
suzu	錫 (すず)	pewter or tin

■ TEXTURE

texture	*tekusuchā*	テクスチャー
feel (against the skin)	*tezawari*	手触り
soft	*yawarakai*	柔らかい
hard	*katai*	硬い
rough/course/uneven	*arai* *zarazara no* *dekoboko no*	荒い ざらざらの 凸凹の
smooth	*nameraka na* *tsuyatsuya shita*	滑らかな つやつやした

■ AMBIENCE/ATMOSPHERE/APPEARANCE

ambience/atmosphere/ mood/feeling	*kanji* *kankaku*	感じ 感覚
attractive/nice-looking	*kakkō (ga) ii*	格好 (が) いい
cute	*kawaii*	かわいい
pretty	*kirei na*	きれいな
beautiful	*utsukushii*	美しい
lovely	*suteki na*	素敵な
stylish	*o-share na*	おしゃれな
bright	*akarui*	明るい

dark	*kurai*	暗い
understatedly elegant	*shibui*	渋い
simple/unsophisticated/ rustic	*soboku na*	素朴な
sober/subdued/plain	*jimi na*	地味な
spectacular/gaudy/ showy/flashy	*hade na*	派手な
visually cluttered/ complex/confusing	*gocha gocha shite iru*	ごちゃごちゃ している

■ CONDITION

condition	*jōtai* *kondishon*	状態 コンディション
damaged	*kizu ga aru*	傷がある
does not work/ out of order	*koshō shite iru*	故障している
broken	*kowarete iru*	壊れている
dilapidated/falling apart	*boro boro da*	ぼろぼろだ
cracked	*hibi ga aru*	ひびがある
chipped	*kakete iru*	欠けている
bent	*magatte iru*	曲がっている
fragile/easily breakable	*kowareyasui*	壊れやすい
durable/sturdy/ reliable/solid	*jōbu na* *shikkari shite iru*	丈夫な しっかりしている
well-made	*yoku dekite iru*	よくできている
long-lasting/ long-wearing	*nagamochi suru/ shiteiru*	長持ちする／ している

TRADITIONAL JAPANESE CULTURE

The words that follow relate to various aspects of traditional Japanese culture, and are likely to come up often in discussions about things to buy.

archery	*kyūdō*	弓道
art of raising miniature trees	*bonsai*	盆栽
Buddhist temple	*o-tera*	お寺
calligraphy	*shodō*	書道
festival	*matsuri*	祭り
flower arrangement	*ikebana*	生け花
incense ceremony	*kōdō*	香道
Japanese form of Buddhism	*zen*	禅
kabuki drama	*kabuki*	歌舞伎
Noh drama, Japan's oldest performing art	*Noh*	能
puppet theater	*bunraku*	文楽
Shinto shrine	*jinja*	神社
tea ceremony	*chanoyu/chadō*	茶の湯/茶道
tray landscapes	*bonkei*	盆景
tray landscapes (of sand and pebbles)	*bonseki*	盆石

THE WORLD OF FLEA MARKETS

The world of flea markets has its own vocabulary. The words below are useful in a number of conversational contexts.

flea market	*nomi no ichi*	蚤の市
antique market	*kottō ichi*	骨董市
auction (where vendors, dealers, and gallery owners buy antiques for resale)	*ōkushon*	オークション
antique (n)	*kottō*	骨董
antique (n)	*kottōhin*	骨董品
Western antique	*antiku/antīku*	アンティク/アンティーク
vendor, dealer	*kottōya/gyōsha*	骨董屋、業者
flea-market organizer	*daihyōsha/sewanin*	代表者 (だいひょうしゃ)/世話人 (せわにん)

The language in this subsection may be used when arranging for packing and shipping of goods, and for several other purposes. If you need to review time, days, months, or dates, refer to the charts at the end of the section.

Packing and Shipping

Ordinarily, the vendor will wrap something you have bought in newspaper and/or put it in a plastic bag without being asked. In the case of heavy or bulky items, a plastic carry-handle (or string tied into a makeshift handle) will usually be attached. If this is not provided, you are right to request that it be done—for free.

Shipping, on the other hand, is usually the responsibility of the buyer, and by no means happens automatically. While overseas shipping is for all intents and purposes out of the question, within Japan it is feasible via any number of private parcel-delivery services, generally referred to (even among foreigners) as *takkyūbin*. Most vendors are willing to ship items, especially larger ones, as long as you are willing to pay the cost (cash upon delivery [*chaku-barai*] is the easiest form of payment) and to wait a few days for the item to arrive.

When the vendor asks for your address, saying something like "*Jūsho o oshiete kudasai*," give it in writing (Romanized Japanese is acceptable). Also, let the vendor know what day(s) and time you will be home to accept the delivery.

Could you wrap [the thing bought] in newspaper?
Shinbunshi ni tsutsunde moraemasu ka?
新聞紙に包んでもらえますか?

Could you put [the thing bought] in a bag?
Fukuro ni irete moraemasu ka?
袋に入れてもらえますか?

Could you put [the thing bought] in a cardboard box?
Danbōru ni irete moraemasu ka?
ダンボールに入れてもらえますか？

Could you attach a carry-handle?
Hakoberu yō ni shite moraemasu ka?
運べるようにしてもらえますか？

Could you ship [the thing bought] via *takkyūbin*?
Takkyūbin de haitatsu shite moraemasu ka?
宅急便で配達してもらえますか？

Holding Things Not Yet Purchased

There are two ways a vendor may hold a purchase. In return for a nonrefundable cash deposit (agreed separately from the purchase price), a vendor may reserve an item for you until an agreed time.

Alternatively, a vendor may agree to hold an item without a deposit, taking the risk that you will not return for it and knowing that he/she might lose the opportunity to sell it to someone else in the meantime.

In the examples below, substitute the time or amount of money as appropriate.

Could you hold [the thing to buy] until _____ (today)?
(Kyō no) _____ *made totte oite moraemasu ka?*
（今日の）_____ まで取っておいてもらえますか？

Could you hold [the thing to buy] until _____ tomorrow?
Ashita no _____ *made totte oite moraemasu ka?*
明日の _____ まで取っておいてもらえますか？

Could you hold [the thing to buy] until _____ the day after tomorrow?

Asatte no _____ made totte oite moraemasu ka?

あさっての _____ まで取っておいてもらえますか?

I'll pay a deposit of _____ yen.

_____ *yen no uchikin o haraimasu.*

_____ 円の内金を払います。

Keeping Things Already Purchased

Most vendors will accommodate a request to keep something you have already purchased until you come back to pick it up, since they rarely move from their spots, anyway. Substitute the time as appropriate.

Could you keep [the thing bought] until _____ (today)?

(Kyō no) _____ made azukatte moraemasu ka?

(今日の) _____ まで預かってもらえますか?

Could you keep [the thing bought] until _____ tomorrow?

Ashita no _____ made azukatte moraemasu ka?

明日の _____ まで預かってもらえますか?

Could you keep [the thing bought] until _____ the day after tomorrow?

Asatte no _____ made azukatte moraemasu ka?

あさっての _____ まで預かってもらえますか?

Finding Out a Vendor's Schedule and Contact Information

Use the language in this section to inquire about a vendor's schedule or to ask for his/her contact information.

Sometimes you will need to come back later to pick up something purchased. You may want to check if the vendor will show up the next time the flea market is held, or you may try to connect with the same vendor at a different venue. Always happy to have customers, vendors will ordinarily give you this information without hesitation.

When asking for a vendor's contact information, it's best to try to get a *meishi* (business card) to save you the trouble of writing down the details one by one. Although some vendors do not have cards, gallery owners and the more "professional" vendors always have them, sometimes even printed in both *kanji* and Romanized Japanese.

Until what time (today) will you be here?
(Kyō wa) nan-ji made imasu ka?
(今日は) 何時までいますか?

At what time (today) will you leave?
(Kyō wa) nan-ji ni kaerimasu ka?
(今日は) 何時に帰りますか?

Will you be at this flea market the next time it is held?
Jikai wa demasu ka?
次回は出ますか?

What is the next flea market in the _____ area you will be at?
_____ *de, tsugi ni doko no nomi no ichi ni demasu ka?*
_____ で、次にどこの蚤の市に出ますか?

May I have your business card?
Meishi ga arimasu ka?
名刺がありますか?

Please tell me your _____ .
_____ *o oshiete kudasai.*
_____ を教えて下さい。

telephone number	*(futsū no) denwa bangō*	(普通の) 電話番号
mobile phone number	*keitai no denwa bangō*	携帯の電話番号
fax number	*fakkusu bangō*	ファックス番号
address	*jūsho*	住所

Time

What time is it?
Nan-ji desu ka?
何時ですか。

It's one o'clock (in the morning).	It's one o'clock (in the afternoon).
(Asa no) ichi-ji desu.	*(Gogo no) ichi-ji desu.*
(朝の) 1時です。	(午後の) 1時です。

It's ten minutes before one.	It's ten minutes past one.
Ichi-ji jup-pun mae desu.	*Ichi-ji jup-pun sugi desu.*
1時10分前です。	1時10分過ぎです。
It's 12:50.	It's 1:10.
Jū-ni-ji go-jup-pun desu.	*Ichi-ji jup-pun desu.*
12時50分です。	1時10分です。

It's half past one.
Ichi-ji-han desu.
1時半です。

It's 1:30.
Ichi-ji san-jup-pun desu.
1時30分です。

HOURS			MINUTES		
1 o'clock	*ichi-ji*	1時	1 minute	*ip-pun*	1分
2 o'clock	*ni-ji*	2時	2 minutes	*ni-fun*	2分
3 o'clock	*san-ji*	3時	3 minutes	*san-pun*	3分
4 o'clock	*yo-ji*	4時	4 minutes	*yon-pun*	4分
5 o'clock	*go-ji*	5時	5 minutes	*go-fun*	5分
6 o'clock	*roku-ji*	6時	10 minutes	*jup-pun*	10分
7 o'clock	*shichi-ji*	7時	15 minutes	*jūgo-fun*	15分
8 o'clock	*hachi-ji*	8時	20 minutes	*nijup-pun*	20分
9 o'clock	*ku-ji*	9時	30 minutes	*sanjup-pun*	30分
10 o'clock	*jū-ji*	10時	40 minutes	*yonjup-pun*	40分
11 o'clock	*jū-ichi-ji*	11時	50 minutes	*gojup-pun*	50分
12 o'clock	*jū-ni-ji*	12時	1 hour	*ichi-jikan*	1時間
What time?	*nan-ji?*	何時	How many minutes?/ What minute?	*nan-pun?*	何分

Days, Months, and Dates

Use this chart to review days, months, and dates.

DAYS

Monday	*getsu-yōbi*	月曜日
Tuesday	*ka-yōbi*	火曜日
Wednesday	*sui-yōbi*	水曜日
Thursday	*moku-yōbi*	木曜日
Friday	*kin-yōbi*	金曜日
Saturday	*do-yōbi*	土曜日
Sunday	*nichi-yōbi*	日曜日
What day?	*nan-yōbi?*	何曜日

MONTHS

January	*ichi-gatsu*	1月
February	*ni-gatsu*	2月
March	*san-gatsu*	3月
April	*shi-gatsu*	4月
May	*go-gatsu*	5月
June	*roku-gatsu*	6月
July	*shichi-gatsu*	7月
August	*hachi-gatsu*	8月
September	*ku-gatsu*	9月
October	*jū-gatsu*	10月
November	*jū-ichi-gatsu*	11月
December	*jū-ni-gatsu*	12月
What month?	*nan-gatsu?*	何月

1st	*tsuitachi*	1日
2nd	*futsu-ka*	2日
3rd	*mik-ka*	3日
4th	*yok-ka*	4日
5th	*itsu-ka*	5日
6th	*mui-ka*	6日
7th	*nano-ka*	7日
8th	*yō-ka*	8日
9th	*kokono-ka*	9日
10th	*tō-ka*	10日
11th	*jū-ichi-nichi*	11日
12th	*jū-ni-nichi*	12日
13th	*jū-san-nichi*	13日
14th	*jū-yok-ka*	14日
15th	*jū-go-nichi*	15日
16th	*jū-roku-nichi*	16日
17th	*jū-shichi-nichi*	17日
18th	*jū-hachi-nichi*	18日
19th	*jū-ku-nichi*	19日
20th	*hatsu-ka*	20日
21st	*ni-jū-ichi-nichi*	21日
22nd	*ni-jū-ni-nichi*	22日
23rd	*ni-jū-san-nichi*	23日
24th	*ni-jū-yok-ka*	24日
25th	*ni-jū-go-nichi*	25日
26th	*ni-jū-roku-nichi*	26日
27th	*ni-jū-shichi-nichi*	27日
28th	*ni-jū-hachi-nichi*	28日
29th	*ni-jū-ku-nichi*	29日
30th	*san-jū-nichi*	30日
31th	*san-jū-ichi-nichi*	31日
What date?	*nan-nichi?*	何日

FLEA MARKETS
CALENDAR

NOTE: The general area (prefecture, region, or large city) for each flea market is indicated in SMALL CAPITALS and is followed by the local city, township, or (for larger cities) ward/district. The number at the end of each listing locates the market the Flea Market Listings found on pages 35 to 76 and the general map of Japan.

WEEKLY SCHEDULE

■ EVERY SUNDAY
Hanazono Jinja Aozora Kottō Ichi   TOKYO, Shinjuku   4

■ 1ST SATURDAY
Iidabashi Ramura Kottō Antique Aozora Ichi   TOKYO, Iidabashi   6
Kiryū Tenmangū Komingu Kottō Ichi   GUNMA, Kiryū-shi   53
Obihiro Komingu Kottō Ichi   HOKKAIDO, Obihiro-shi   77
Sagami Nomi no Ichi   KANAGAWA, Atsugi   35
Shinmeigū Garakuta Ichi   TOKYO, Asagaya   19
Tanashi Jinja Aozora Kottō Ichi   OUTLYING TOKYO, Tanashi   21

■ 1ST SUNDAY
Arai Yakushi Kottō Ichi (except January)   TOKYO, Nakano-ku   15
Gokoku Jinja Kita no Nomi no Ichi (December–March)
   HOKKAIDO, Sapporo-shi   75

Hannō Fukurō Ichi SAITAMA, Hannō-shi 45

Obihiro Komingu Kottō Ichi HOKKAIDO, Obihiro-shi 77

Shōnan Kottō Nomi no Ichi KANAGAWA, Fujisawa 32

Sumadera Nomi no Ichi KOBE, Suma-ku 70

Suwa Jinja Komingu Kottō Ichi YAMAGATA, Yamagata-shi 79

Takasaki Tamachi Kottō Kaidō GUNMA, Takasaki-shi 51

Tōgane Kottō matsuri CHIBA, Tōgane-shi 39

Tōgō no Mori Nomi no Ichi TOKYO, Harajuku 3

Tōji Garakuta Ichi KYOTO, Minami-ku 55

Tomioka Hachiman Kottō Ichi TOKYO, Monzen Nakachō 14

Toyama Aozora Nomi no Ichi TOYAMA, Toyama-shi 101

Yamaguchi Flea Market Kottō Ichi YAMAGUCHI, Yamaguchi-shi 107

■ 1ST FRIDAY
O-hatsu Tenjin Nomi no Ichi OSAKA, Kita-ku 61

■ 2ND SATURDAY
Higashi Fushimi Eki-mae Kottō Ichi (April–December)
OUTLYING TOKYO, Higashi Fushimi 20

■ 2ND SUNDAY
Arai Yakushi Kottō Ichi (January only) TOKYO, Nakano-ku 15

Fussa Shichi Fukujin Takara Ichi OUTLYING TOKYO, Fussa-shi 26

Kōriyama Nomi no Ichi NARA, Yamato Kōriyama-shi 71

Miwa Jinja Tōzai Kobutsu Kottō Ichi NARA, Sakurai-shi 72

Nogi Jinja Komingu Kottō Ichi (except November)
TOKYO, Nogizaka 1

Ogushi Jinja Nomi no Ichi (except November)
SHIZUOKA, Shizuoka-shi 91

Okegawa-shi Furusato Nomi no Ichi SAITAMA, Okegawa-shi 43

Ōsaki Jinja O-takara Kottō Ichi (except November)
TOCHIGI, Mooka-shi 47

Tomioka Hachiman Kottō Ichi TOKYO, Monzen Nakachō 14

Yasukuni Jinja Aozora Kottō Ichi (July only, 2nd or 3rd Sunday)
TOKYO, Kudan 10

Yonezawa Machi no Hiroba Komingu Kottō Nomi no Ichi
(April–November) YAMAGATA, Yonezawa-shi 80

■ 2ND MONDAY

Higashi Fushimi Eki-mae Kottō Ichi (January–March)
  OUTLYING TOKYO, Higashi Fushimi 20

■ 3RD SATURDAY

Obiki Inari Kottō Ichi GUNMA, Tatebayashi-shi 54

Yamato Promenade Komingu Kottō Ichi KANAGAWA, Yamato-shi 34

■ 3RD SUNDAY

Chiba Dera Kottō Ichi CHIBA, Chiba-shi 36

Hakushima Nomi No Ichi HIROSHIMA, Hiroshima-shi 104

Koedo Hikone no Kottō Ichi SHIGA, Hikone-shi 74

Kuri no Ie Nomi no Ichi IBARAKI, Iwama 49

Ogushi Jinja Nomi no Ichi (in November only)
  SHIZUOKA, Shizuoka-shi 91

Sendai Daikannon Komingu Kottō Ichi MIYAGI, Sendai-shi 82

Shigisan Tora no Ichi NARA, Ikoma-gun 73

Takahata Fudō Gozare Ichi OUTLYING TOKYO, Hino-shi 23

Tatsu no Kuchi Dai Kottō Ichi KANAGAWA, Enoshima 31

Yasukuni Jinja Aozora Kottō Ichi (July only, 2nd or 3rd Sunday)
  TOKYO, Kudan 10

■ 3RD FRIDAY

O-hatsu Tenjin Nomi no Ichi OSAKA, Kita-ku 61

■ 4TH SATURDAY

Futaara Kottō Ichi TOCHIGI, Utsunomiya-shi 46

Kishibojin Kottō Ichi TOKYO, Ikebukuro 5

Kyūshū Kottō Matsuri (Jan, Mar, May, July, Sept, Nov)
  KAGOSHIMA, Kagoshima-shi 112

Mishima Taisha Kottō Matsuri SHIZUOKA, Mishima-shi 90

Ōmiya Hachimangū Komingu Kottō Ichi TOKYO, Eifukuchō 17

Tōri-machi Shōfuku Inari Kottō Ichi (April–October)
  AKITA, Akita-shi 78

Urawa Juku Furusato Ichi SAITAMA, Urawa-shi 40

■ **4TH SUNDAY**

Bazaar in Rokkō   KOBE, Nada-ku   68

Hachiōji Sengen Jinja Silk Road Mukashi Ichi
   OUTLYING TOKYO, Hachiōji   24

Hikawa Jinja Kottō Ichi   TOKYO, Shakujii   16

Ichinoya Yasaka Jinja Kottō Nomi No Ichi   IBARAKI, Tsukuba-shi   48

Kyūshū Kottō Matsuri (Jan, Mar, May, July, Sept, Nov)
   KAGOSHIMA, Kagoshima-shi   112

Makuhari Kottō Ichi   CHIBA, Makuhari   38

Mishima Taisha Kottō Matsuri   SHIZUOKA, Mishima-shi   90

Ōmiya Hachimangū Komingu Kottō Ichi   TOKYO, Eifukuchō   17

Ōsaki Jinja O-takara Kottō Ichi (November only)
   TOCHIGI, Mooka-shi   47

Sendai Komingu Kottō Aozora Ichi   MIYAGI, Sendai-shi   83

Shōnan Kottō Nomi no Ichi   KANAGAWA, Fujisawa-shi   32

Sumiyoshi Square Kottō Ichi   HIROSHIMA, Fukuyama-shi   106

Tōgō no Mori Nomi no Ichi   TOKYO, Harajuku   3

■ **4TH MONDAY**

Mishima Taisha Kottō Matsuri   SHIZUOKA, Mishima-shi   90

■ **4TH THURSDAY, 4TH FRIDAYS**

Roppongi Antique Fair   TOKYO, Roppongi   2

■ **LAST SUNDAY, EXCEPT DECEMBER**

Nandemo Yokka no Ichi   MIE, Yokka-ichi-shi   97

■ **LAST SATURDAY, SUNDAY, MONDAY OF MARCH & SEPTEMBER**

Gifu Kottō Matsuri   GIFU, Gifu-shi   98

■ **LAST SUNDAY (APRIL–NOVEMBER)**

Toyohira Jinja Kottō Aozora Ichi   HOKKAIDO, Sapporo-shi   76

JANUARY

1–3	**Kottō Festa in Hamamatsu** SHIZUOKA, Hamamatsu-shi 93
1–4	**Tōji Shōgatsu Ichi** KYOTO, Minami-ku 57
around New Year's	**Echizen Kottō Matsuri** FUKUI, Fukui-shi (4 days) 103
5th	**Hōshu no Ichi** KANAGAWA, Tsujidō 33
8th	**Ikutama Nomi no Ichi** OSAKA, Tennōji-ku 62
	Machida Tenmangū Garakuta Kottō Ichi OUTLYING TOKYO, Machida-shi 27
9th	**Kogane Jinja Kottō Ichi** GIFU, Gifu-shi 99
15–16	**Setagaya Boro Ichi** TOKYO, Setagaya-ku 18
18th	**Ōsu Kannon Kottō Ichi** AICHI, Nagoya-shi 96
21st	**Shitennōji Daisi-e** OSAKA, Tennōji-ku 63
	Tōji Kōbō Ichi KYOTO, Minami-ku 56
25th	**Chōfu Tenjin Ichi** OUTLYING TOKYO, Chōfu-shi 22
	Dōmyōji Tenmangū Nomi no Ichi OSAKA, Fujiidera-shi 66
	Kitano Tenmangū Tenjin Ichi KYOTO, Kamigyō-ku 58
28th	**Kawagoe Narita Fudō Nomi no Ichi** SAITAMA, Kawagoe-shi 41
	Koedo Kawagoe Charity Kottō Ichi SAITAMA, Kawagoe-shi 42
	Ōsu Kannon Kottō Ichi AICHI, Nagoya-shi 96

FEBRUARY

1st	**Machida Tenmangū Garakuta Kottō Ichi** OUTLYING TOKYO, Machida-shi 27
5th	**Hōshu no Ichi** KANAGAWA, Tsujidō 33
8th	**Ikutama Nomi no Ichi** OSAKA, Tennōji-ku 62
9th	**Kogane Jinja Kottō Ichi** GIFU, Gifu-shi 99

18th	Ōsu Kannon Kottō Ichi AICHI, Nagoya-shi 96
21st	Shitennōji Daisi-e OSAKA, Tennōji-ku 63
	Tōji Kōbō Ichi KYOTO, Minami-ku 56
25th	Chōfu Tenjin Ichi OUTLYING TOKYO, Chōfu-shi 22
	Dōmyōji Tenmangū Nomi no Ichi OSAKA, Fujiidera-shi 66
	Kitano Tenmangū Tenjin Ichi KYOTO, Kamigyō-ku 58
28th	Kawagoe Narita Fudō Nomi no Ichi SAITAMA, Kawagoe-shi 41
	Koedo Kawagoe Charity Kottō Ichi SAITAMA, Kawagoe-shi 42
	Ōsu Kannon Kotto Ichi AICHI, Nagoya-shi 96
February (2 days)	Kottō Antique Fair KANAGAWA, Yokohama 28
	Sekai Kottō Fair in Osaka Dome OSAKA, Nishi-ku 65
February (3 days)	Chūgoku Shikoku Kottōhin Tenji Sokubaikai, Sanuki Kottō Ichi KAGAWA, Takamatsu-shi 115
	Maebashi Zenkoku Kottō Nomi no Ichi GUNMA, Maebashi-shi 52
	Terukuni Jinja Nomi no Ichi KAGOSHIMA, Kagoshima-shi 114
February or March (3 days)	Heiwajima Zenkoku Komingu Kottō Matsuri TOKYO, Heiwajima 11
	Shinshū Kottō Haku NAGANO, Matsumoto-shi 89

MARCH

1st	Machida Tenmangū Garakuta Kottō Ichi OUTLYING TOKYO, Machida-shi 27
5th	Hōshu no Ichi KANAGAWA, Tsujidō 33
8th	Ikutama Nomi no Ichi OSAKA, Tennōji-ku 62
9th	Kogane Jinja Kottō Ichi GIFU, Gifu-shi 99
18th	Ōsu Kannon Kottō Ichi AICHI, Nagoya-shi 96

APRIL

18th	Ōsu Kannon Kottō Ichi AICHI, Nagoya-shi 96
21st	Shitennōji Daisi-e OSAKA, Tennōji-ku 63
	Tōji Kōbō Ichi KYOTO, Minami-ku 56
25th	Chōfu Tenjin Ichi OUTLYING TOKYO, Chōfu-shi 22
	Dōmyōji Tenmangū Nomi no Ichi OSAKA, Fujiidera-shi 66
	Kitano Tenmangū Tenjin Ichi KYOTO, Kamigyō-ku 58
28th	Kawagoe Narita Fudō Nomi no Ichi SAITAMA, Kawagoe-shi 41
	Koedo Kawagoe Charity Kottō Ichi SAITAMA, Kawagoe-shi 42
	Ōsu Kannon Kottō Ichi AICHI, Nagoya-shi 96
April (3 days)	Nagoya Kokusai Antique and Kottō Ichi AICHI, Nagoya-shi 94
	Osaka Kottō Matsuri OSAKA, Chūō-ku 64
	Takasaki Zenkoku Kottō Nomi no Ichi GUNMA, Takasaki-shi 50

MAY

1st	Machida Tenmangū Garakuta Kottō Ichi OUTLYING TOKYO, Machida-shi 27
5th	Hōshu no Ichi KANAGAWA, Tsujidō 33
7th	Hida Takayama Garakuta Ichi GIFU, Takayama-shi 100
8th	Ikutama Nomi no Ichi OSAKA, Tennōji-ku 62
9th	Kogane Jinja Kottō Ichi GIFU, Gifu-shi 99
18th	Ōsu Kannon Kottō Ichi AICHI, Nagoya-shi 96
21st	Shitennōji Daisi-e OSAKA, Tennōji-ku 63
	Tōji Kōbō Ichi KYOTO, Minami-ku 56
25th	Chōfu Tenjin Ichi OUTLYING TOKYO, Chōfu-shi 22
	Dōmyōji Tenmangū Nomi no Ichi OSAKA, Fujiidera-shi 66
	Kitano Tenmangū Tenjin Ichi KYOTO, Kamigyo-ku 58

28th	**Kawagoe Narita Fudō Nomi no Ichi**
	Saitama, Kawagoe-shi 41
	Koedo Kawagoe Charity Kottō Ichi
	Saitama, Kawagoe-shi 42
	Ōsu Kannon Kottō Ichi Aichi, Nagoya-shi 96
May (2 days)	**Dazaifu Tenjin Omoshiro Ichi**
	Fukuoka, Dazaifu-shi 108
May (3 days)	**Akishima Kottō Antique Fair**
	Outlying Tokyo, Akishima-shi 25
	Heiwajima Zenkoku Komingu Kottō Matsuri
	Tokyo, Heiwajima 11
	Kottō and Antique in Fukuoka
	Fukuoka, Fukuoka-shi 109
	Nagoya Kottō Matsuri Aichi, Nagoya-shi 95
	Tokyo Dome Prism Kottō Fair Tokyo, Kōrakuen 7

June

1st	**Machida Tenmangū Garakuta Kottō Ichi**
	Outlying Tokyo, Machida-shi 27
5th	**Hōshu no Ichi** Kanagawa, Tsujidō 33
7th	**Hida Takayama Garakuta Ichi** Gifu, Takayama-shi 100
8th	**Ikutama Nomi no Ichi** Osaka, Tennōji-ku 62
9th	**Kogane Jinja Kottō Ichi** Gifu, Gifu-shi 99
18th	**Ōsu Kannon Kottō Ichi** Aichi, Nagoya-shi 96
21st	**Shitennōji Daisi-e** Osaka, Tennōji-ku 63
	Tōji Kōbō Ichi Kyoto, Minami-ku 56
25th	**Chōfu Tenjin Ichi** Outlying Tokyo, Chōfu-shi 22
	Dōmyōji Tenmangū Nomi no Ichi
	Osaka, Fujiidera-shi 66
	Kitano Tenmangū Tenjin Ichi Kyoto, Kamigyō-ku 58
28th	**Kawagoe Narita Fudō Nomi no Ichi**
	Saitama, Kawagoe-shi 41

June (3 days)	**Koedo Kawagoe Charity Kottō Ichi** SAITAMA, Kawagoe-shi 42
	Ōsu Kannon Kottō Ichi AICHI, Nagoya-shi 96
	Chūgoku Shikoku Kottōhin Tenji Sokubaikai, **Sanuki Kottō Ichi** KAGAWA, Takamatsu-shi 115
	Heiwajima Zenkoku Komingu Kottō Matsuri TOKYO, Heiwajima 11
	Kyoto Dai Kottō Matsuri KYOTO, Fushimi-ku 59

JULY

5th	**Hōshu no Ichi** KANAGAWA, Tsujidō 33
7th	**Hida Takayama Garakuta Ichi** GIFU, Takayama-shi 100
8th	**Ikutama Nomi no Ichi** OSAKA, Tennōji-ku 62
9th	**Kogane Jinja Kottō Ichi** GIFU, Gifu-shi 99
July 17– August 10, daily	**Ueno Natsu Matsuri Yoru no Kottō Ichi** TOKYO, Ueno 9
18th	**Ōsu Kannon Kottō Ichi** AICHI, Nagoya-shi 96
21st	**Shitennōji Daisi-e** OSAKA, Tennōji-ku 63
	Tōji Kōbō Ichi KYOTO, Minami-ku 56
25th	**Chōfu Tenjin Ichi** OUTLYING TOKYO, Chōfu-shi 22
	Dōmyōji Tenmangū Nomi no Ichi OSAKA, Fujiidera-shi 66
	Kitano Tenmangū Tenjin Ichi KYOTO, Kamigyō-ku 58
28th	**Kawagoe Narita Fudō Nomi no Ichi** SAITAMA, Kawagoe-shi 41
	Koedo Kawagoe Charity Kottō Ichi SAITAMA, Kawagoe-shi 42
	Ōsu Kannon Kottō Ichi AICHI, Nagoya-shi 96
July (2 days)	**Dazaifu Tenjin Omoshiro Ichi** FUKUOKA, Dazaifu-shi 108
July (3 days)	**Kottō Antique Fair in Makuhari Messe** CHIBA, Makuhari 37

	Osaka Kottō Matsuri OSAKA, Chūō-ku 64
	Sendai Zenkoku Kottō Nomi no Ichi MIYAGI, Sendai-shi 84
	Twin Messe Shizuoka, Nagoya Kottō Matsuri SHIZUOKA, Shizuoka-shi 92
July (2nd or 3rd Sunday)	Machida Tenmangū Garakuta Kottō Ichi OUTLYING TOKYO, Machida-shi 27

AUGUST

1–31	Karuizawa Natsu no Nomi No Ichi NAGANO, Karuizawa-machi 88
July 17– August 10, daily	Ueno Natsu Matsuri Yoru no Kottō Ichi TOKYO, Ueno 9
1st	Machida Tenmangū Garakuta Kottō Ichi OUTLYING TOKYO, Machida-shi 27
5th	Hōshu no Ichi KANAGAWA, Tsujidō 33
7th	Hida Takayama Garakuta Ichi GIFU, Takayama-shi 100
8th	Ikutama Nomi no Ichi OSAKA, Tennōji-ku 62
9th	Kogane Jinja Kottō Ichi GIFU, Gifu-shi 99
13–15	Kottō Festa in Hamamatsu SHIZUOKA, Hamamatsu-shi 93
18th	Ōsu Kannon Kottō Ichi AICHI, Nagoya-shi 96
21st	Shitennōji Daisi-e OSAKA, Tennōji-ku 63
	Tōji Kōbō Ichi KYOTO, Minami-ku 56
25th	Chōfu Tenjin Ichi OUTLYING TOKYO, Chōfu-shi 22
	Dōmyōji Tenmangū Nomi no Ichi OSAKA, Fujiidera-shi 66
	Kitano Tenmangū Tenjin Ichi KYOTO, Kamigyō-ku 58
28th	Kawagoe Narita Fudō Nomi no Ichi SAITAMA, Kawagoe-shi 41
	Koedo Kawagoe Charity Kottō Ichi SAITAMA, Kawagoe-shi 42
	Ōsu Kannon Kottō Ichi AICHI, Nagoya-shi 96

August (3 days)	**Maebashi Zenkoku Kottō Nomi no Ichi** GUNMA, Maebashi-shi 52
	Nagoya Kottō Matsuri AICHI, Nagoya-shi 95
August (4 days around O-bon, 8/15)	**Echizen Kottō Matsuri** FUKUI, Fukui-shi 103

SEPTEMBER

1st	**Machida Tenmangū Garakuta Kottō Ichi** OUTLYING TOKYO, Machida-shi 27
5th	**Hōshu no Ichi** KANAGAWA, Tsujidō 33
7th	**Hida Takayama Garakuta Ichi** GIFU, Takayama-shi 100
8th	**Ikutama Nomi no Ichi** OSAKA, Tennōji-ku 62
9th	**Kogane Jinja Kottō Ichi** GIFU, Gifu-shi 99
18th	**Ōsu Kannon Kottō Ichi** AICHI, Nagoya-shi 96
21st	**Shitennōji Daisi-e** OSAKA, Tennōji-ku 63
	Tōji Kōbō Ichi KYOTO, Minami-ku 56
25th	**Chōfu Tenjin Ichi** OUTLYING TOKYO, Chōfu-shi 22
	Dōmyōji Tenmangū Nomi no Ichi OSAKA, Fujiidera-shi 66
	Kitano Tenmangū Tenjin Ichi KYOTO, Kamigyō-ku 58
28th	**Kawagoe Narita Fudō Nomi no Ichi** SAITAMA, Kawagoe-shi 41
	Koedo Kawagoe Charity Kottō Ichi SAITAMA, Kawagoe-shi 42
	Ōsu Kannon Kottō Ichi AICHI, Nagoya-shi 96
September (2 days)	**Aya Shusen no Mori Kottō Nomi no Ichi** MIYAZAKI, Aya-shi 110
	Dazaifu Tenjin Omoshiro Ichi FUKUOKA, Dazaifu-shi 108
	Kottō Antique Fair KANAGAWA, Yokohama 28
September (3 days)	**Heiwajima Zenkoku Komingu Kottō Matsuri** TOKYO, Heiwajima 11

Kottō and Antique in Fukuoka
FUKUOKA, Fukuoka-shi 109

Niigata Kottō Ōichi NIIGATA, Niigata-shi 87

OCTOBER

1–31	Ueno Koen Aki no Kottō Matsuri TOKYO, Ueno 8
1st	Machida Tenmangū Garakuta Kottō Ichi OUTLYING TOKYO, Machida-shi 27
5th	Hōshu no Ichi KANAGAWA, Tsujidō 33
7th	Hida Takayama Garakuta Ichi GIFU, Takayama-shi 100
8th	Ikutama Nomi no Ichi OSAKA, Tennōji-ku 62
9th	Kogane Jinja Kottō Ichi GIFU, Gifu-shi 99
18th	Ōsu Kannon Kottō Ichi AICHI, Nagoya-shi 96
21st	Shitennōji Daisi-e OSAKA, Tennōji-ku 63
	Tōji Kōbō Ichi KYOTO, Minami-ku 56
25th	Chōfu Tenjin Ichi OUTLYING TOKYO, Chōfu-shi 22
	Dōmyōji Tenmangū Nomi no Ichi OSAKA, Fujiidera-shi 66
	Kitano Tenmangū Tenjin Ichi KYOTO, Kamigyō-ku 58
28th	Kawagoe Narita Fudō Nomi no Ichi SAITAMA, Kawagoe-shi 41
	Koedo Kawagoe Charity Kottō Ichi SAITAMA, Kawagoe-shi 42
	Ōsu Kannon Kottō Ichi AICHI, Nagoya-shi 96
October (2 days)	Dazaifu Tenjin Omoshiro Ichi FUKUOKA, Dazaifu-shi 108
October (3 days)	Osaka Kottō Matsuri OSAKA, Chūō-ku 64
October or November (3 days)	Shinshū Kottō Haku NAGANO, Matsumoto-shi 89

1st	**Machida Tenmangū Garakuta Kottō Ichi** OUTLYING TOKYO, Machida-shi 27
5th	**Hōshu no Ichi** KANAGAWA, Tsujidō 33
8th	**Ikutama Nomi no Ichi** OSAKA, Tennōji-ku 62
9th	**Kogane Jinja Kottō Ichi** GIFU, Gifu-shi 99
18th	**Ōsu Kannon Kottō Ichi** AICHI, Nagoya-shi 96
21st	**Shitennōji Daisi-e** OSAKA, Tennōji-ku 63
	Tōji Kōbō Ichi KYOTO, Minami-ku 56
25th	**Chōfu Tenjin Ichi** OUTLYING TOKYO, Chōfu-shi 22
	Dōmyōji Tenmangū Nomi no Ichi OSAKA, Fujiidera-shi 66
	Kitano Tenmangū Tenjin Ichi KYOTO, Kamigyō-ku 58
28th	**Kawagoe Narita Fudō Nomi no Ichi** SAITAMA, Kawagoe-shi 41
	Koedo Kawagoe Charity Kottō Ichi SAITAMA, Kawagoe-shi 42
	Ōsu Kannon Kottō Ichi AICHI, Nagoya-shi 96
November (3 days)	**Akishima Kottō Antique Fair** TOKYO, Akishima-shi 25
	Chūgoku Shikoku Kottōhin Tenji Sokubaikai, **Sanuki Kottō Ichi** KAGAWA, Takamatsu-shi 115
	Echigo Nagaoka Kottō Ōichi NIIGATA, Nagaoka-shi 86
	Kottō and Antique in Hiroshima HIROSHIMA, Hiroshima-shi 105
	Kyoto Dai Kottō Matsuri KYOTO, Fushimi-ku 59
	Nagoya Kokusai Antique and Kottō Ichi AICHI, Nagoya-shi 94
	Sendai Zenkoku Kottō Nomi no Ichi MIYAGI, Sendai-shi 84
	Tokyo Dome Prism Kottō Fair TOKYO, Korakuen 7
	Yokohama Kottō World KANAGAWA, Yokohama 30
October or November (3 days)	**Shinshū Kottō Haku** NAGANO, Matsumoto-shi 89

1st	**Machida Tenmangū Garakuta Kottō Ichi** OUTLYING TOKYO, Machida-shi 27
5th	**Hōshu no Ichi** KANAGAWA, Tsujidō 33
8th	**Ikutama Nomi no Ichi** OSAKA, Tennōji-ku 62
9th	**Kogane Jinja Kottō Ichi** GIFU, Gifu-shi 99
15–16	**Setagaya Boro Ichi** TOKYO, Setagaya-ku 18
18th	**Ōsu Kannon Kottō Ichi** AICHI, Nagoya-shi 96
21st	**Shitennōji Daisi-e** OSAKA, Tennōji-ku 63
	Tōji Kōbō Ichi KYOTO, Minami-ku 56
25th	**Chōfu Tenjin Ichi** OUTLYING TOKYO, Chōfu-shi 22
	Dōmyōji Tenmangū Nomi no Ichi OSAKA, Fujiidera-shi 66
	Kitano Tenmangū Tenjin Ichi KYOTO, Kamigyō-ku 58
28th	**Kawagoe Narita Fudō Nomi no Ichi** SAITAMA, Kawagoe-shi 41
	Koedo Kawagoe Charity Kottō Ichi SAITAMA, Kawagoe-shi 42
	Ōsu Kannon Kottō Ichi AICHI, Nagoya-shi 96
December (2 days)	**Dazaifu Tenjin Omoshiro Ichi** FUKUOKA, Dazaifu-shi 108
December (3 days)	**Heiwajima Zenkoku Komingu Kottō Matsuri** TOKYO, Heiwajima 11
	Nagoya Kottō Matsuri AICHI, Nagoya-shi 95
	Takasaki Zenkoku Kottō Nomi no Ichi GUNMA, Takasaki-shi 50
	Twin Messe Shizuoka, Nagoya Kottō Matsuri SHIZUOKA, Shizuoka-shi 92

5 or 6 times a year (2 days each)	**Satsuma Nana-ju-nana-man-goku Kottō Matsuri** KAGOSHIMA, Kagoshima-shi 113
4 or 5 times a year (2 days each)	**Kottō Nomi no Ichi Matsuri in Miyazaki** MIYAZAKI, Miyazaki-shi 111
Spring (2 days), fall (2 days)	**Sakai Dai Kottō Matsuri** OSAKA, Sakai-shi 67
	Sendai Charity Komingu Kottō Ichi MIYAGI, Sendai-shi 81
Spring (3 days), fall (3 days)	**Kanazawa Kottō Matsuri** ISHIKAWA, Kanazawa-shi 102
	Kobe Dai Kottō Matsuri KOBE, Higashi Nada-ku 69
	Kōriyama Kobijutsu Kottō Ichi FUKUSHIMA, Kōriyama-shi 85
	Kottō and Antique Tenji Sokubaikai TOKYO, Hamamatsuchō 12
	Sai no Kuni Wayō Kottō Fair in Tokorozawa SAITAMA, Tokorozawa-shi 44
	Yokohama Kottō Ichi KANAGAWA, Yokohama 29
Summer (3 days), winter (3 days)	**Kottō Jamboree** TOKYO, Odaiba 13
	Zenkoku Kottōya Daishūgō in Kyoto KYOTO, Fushimi-ku 60

INDEX OF FLEA MARKETS

NOTE: The general area (prefecture, region, or large city) for each flea market is indicated in SMALL CAPITALS and is followed by the local city, township, or (for larger cities) ward/district. The number at the end of each listing locates the market the Flea Market Listings found on pages 35 to 76 and the general map of Japan.

THINGS TO BUY

Alphabetical Listing

日本「のみの市」ガイド
FLEA MARKETS OF JAPAN

2003 年 1 月 10 日　第 1 刷発行

著　者　セオドア・マニング

発行者　畑野文夫

発行所　講談社インターナショナル株式会社
　　　　〒112-8652 東京都文京区音羽 1-17-14
　　　　電話　03-3944-6493（編集部）
　　　　　　　03-3944-6492（営業部・業務部）
　　　　ホームページ　http://www.kodansha-intl.co.jp

印刷所　大日本印刷株式会社

製本所　株式会社国宝社

落丁本・乱丁本は購入書店名を明記のうえ、小社業務部宛にお送りください。
送料小社負担にてお取替えします。なお、この本についてのお問い合わせ
は、編集部宛にお願いいたします。本書の無断複写（コピー）、転載は著作権
法の例外を除き、禁じられています。

定価はカバーに表示してあります。

© セオドア・マニング 2003
Printed in Japan
ISBN 4-7700-2902-0